Hotels

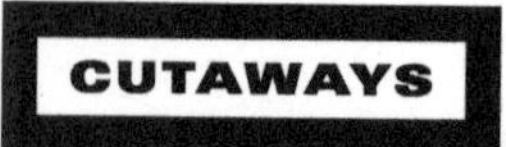

SERIES EDITORS:
Erika Balsom (King's College London) and **Genevieve Yue** (The New School)

"This new series of small-format books focused on cinematic motifs, themes, and devices represents something new and exciting in English-language writing on film" —**Dennis Lim, Artistic Director, New York Film Festival**

"Featuring some of the field's most exciting scholars and critics, Cutaways is a welcome addition to film writing. The series promises to expand the ways cinema is conceived, consumed, and received, in ways that parallel the contemporary situation of cinema." —**Sarah Keller, author of *Anxious Cinephilia: Pleasure and Peril at the Movies***

Cutaways is a series of pocket-sized books by and for movie lovers. Each volume offers a journey through the history of cinema guided by a single motif or formal device. Featuring original writing by film scholars and critics, the books create a space for intellectually engaged and broadly accessible cinephilia.

Hotels

Jules O'Dwyer

FORDHAM UNIVERSITY PRESS NEW YORK 2025

Fordham University Press also publishes its books in a variety of electronic formats. Some content that appears in print may not be available in electronic books.

Visit us online at www.fordhampress.com.

Library of Congress Cataloging-in-Publication Data available online at https://catalog.loc.gov.

Printed in the United States of America
27 26 25   5 4 3 2 1
First edition

Contents

Hotels

1

I Can't Sleep

A nondescript hotel room: Vienna, 2022. Unable to sleep, I began to speculate about the bodies that occupied the neighboring room. My thoughts telescoped outward, first to consider those in the rooms directly above—the source of loud but irregular thudding movements—and then to consider the housekeepers and the twenty-four-hour reception staff. What better object of contemplation for the restless mind than the space of a hotel, where the competing rhythms of work and rest, labor and laziness, shift work and sleep, and coming and going are all housed under a single roof? Hotels play host to "the congress of the insomniacs," to cite Charles Simic's poem by that name.[1] So if I couldn't sleep, then at least I could console myself with the knowledge that somebody out there was probably sharing the same fate.

In *Hotel Theory*, Wayne Koestenbaum writes in a characteristically epigrammatic style, "To be in hotel is to float."[2] In the hotel, the act of "checking in" is often a kind of checking out; as guests hand over their bags, they are invited to take a brief leave of absence from the stresses, labors, and material heft that otherwise characterize their everyday experience. One person's holiday baggage, however, is another person's workload, even if the architectural arrangements of many hotels try their best to make sure the spheres of labor and leisure do not meet. Hotels both contain and concentrate oppositions between work and play, public and private. While some flaunt the conspicuous signs of their historicity, they can often feel oddly—or even hauntingly—atemporal. Hotels, moreover, are often caught between wanting to emphasize their local specificity while also reminding their guests that they form a crucial node in a global imaginary.

The following pages are concerned with the intertwined histories of the hotel and the cinema—two spaces of social, spatial, and aesthetic mediation that are also routinely held up as emblems of modernity. Both, I argue, are hyperaesthetic spaces that appeal to experiential logics of fantasy, immersion, and aspiration. Both also negotiate our encounters with cultural difference and the outside world (either the "world" presented onscreen or the one that exists beyond the lobby's revolving door). Given the multiplicity of adjacent social spaces contained within the hotel, this setting is ripe for an exploration of cinema's forms and narratives in distinctly spatial terms.

Turning to a wide array of examples, I take a trip through the history of cinema via the interior spaces of hospitality—not only the hotel but also its diminutive cousins: the inn, the motel, and other sites of temporary dwelling that often feature on the big screen. Given the hotel's ubiquity in cinema, such a travel itinerary is one that will take us far afield, from the grand hotels of early twentieth-century Europe to the motels of suburban Florida, from a temporary art installation in Rotterdam to the intercontinental complexes of Tokyo and

Mexico City. Unlike the more exhaustive of travel maps, though, this book does not aspire to completeness. While the size of this book in a sense relieves me of the need to be comprehensive, I should apologize in advance if this book baits its readership with the promise of a lengthy exploration of the Bates Motel in Hitchcock's *Psycho* or if the Overlook Hotel that stands at the center of Kubrick's *The Shining* goes—well—overlooked as I gravitate toward objects that have been less thoroughly parsed.

In what follows, I join scholars, including John David Rhodes (who writes on the house), Pamela Robertson Wojcik (the apartment), and Merrill Schleier (the skyscraper), who collectively assert that while we are not always accustomed to paying attention to the interior spaces we are asked to inhabit when watching a movie, film settings shape our spectatorial encounters in ways that are both striking and subtle.[3] In tandem with this rich body of architectural thinking, I ask: How might cinema's spaces and settings emerge from the backdrop of narrative insignificance to which they are habitually relegated to assume an expressive function? How does the built environment on screen actively scaffold a film's political, aesthetic, and narrative possibilities? And why does the space of the hotel, more particularly, circulate so widely in the cinematic imaginary? To set in motion this book's exploration, let's start by taking a concrete—or rather, brick and mortar—example.

* * *

Return to Vienna. By now in the grip of insomnia, my mind turned toward Claire Denis's 1994 film *I Can't Sleep* (*J'ai pas sommeil*), no doubt on account of the fact that it was set in a hotel with a similar feel and because its title named my affliction at that moment. And with the passing of time and thought I came to inhabit a more liminal space at the cusp of waking and sleeping, an associative state of half-dreaming evocative of the cinematic experience. I started to think about the fault lines and tensions that belie the hotel's ostentatious facade and the work that underpins its slick operation.

I Can't Sleep is set in Paris in the late 1980s. More specifically, it is set in the capital's storied eighteenth arrondissement. By drawing on the experiences of its majority immigrant inhabitants, Denis's film works against the well-worn clichés that tourists associate with this Parisian district: the Moulin Rouge below, the village square above, the long art-historical association with the Belle Epoque and the emerging modernisms of the twentieth century. The film charts the fortunes of Daïga, a Lithuanian immigrant who moves to Paris for a better life following the gradual demise of the Eastern Bloc. Although initially lured to the city by a sleazy film executive with vague promises of acting work, the reality of her day-to-day life is a lot less glamorous. She earns her keep as a chambermaid in a hotel that is run by Ninon, a Slavic woman who is a friend of her aunt. We are introduced to Ninon while she is running self-defense classes for older women. The class is a practical response to a fear that enveloped Paris at the time because of the "Granny Killer," a serial murderer who terrorized the streets of Montmartre in the late 1980s. The identity of the killer is later revealed to be a calm, gentle, queer-coded man named Camille, who also happens to rent a room in Ninon's hotel. Originally from Martinique, Camille turns tricks, moonlights as a drag artist in a subterranean cabaret, and robs and kills elderly women with increasing frequency following his recent HIV diagnosis. All of this is to say: Camille is associated with a string of sensational signifiers. As with the real-life Thierry Paulin, upon whom the character is based, he is an avatar for the overlapping set of anxieties stoked by the French political right at the time. Yet in a markedly unsensational manner, *I Can't Sleep* explores the interlinked trajectory of the two hotel dwellers: Daïga and Camille, both of whom eke out a precarious existence in a hostile political climate. Through the film's aleatory structure, Denis choreographs the errant trajectories of these two characters, which overlap only briefly, inviting us to think about the tenuous forms of community that are forged through a shared sense of estrangement.

In spite of the magnetic, ethereal presence of Daïga and Camille, I have always been struck by the ambivalent space that the hotel occupies in the film. It is a contradictory space of political refuge and arduous labor, one of psychological opacity and voyeuristic transgression. Settings in cinema are often treated as a neutral backdrop against which action transpires; this is especially so when they are not so aesthetically remarkable. The film's shooting location, the Bellevue et du Chariot d'Or, is an unimposing three-star hotel that is not actually in Montmartre but on the Rue Turbigo, a little closer to Paris's center. A late nineteenth-century building, it is shorn of the conspicuous signs of luxury we would associate with neighboring grand hotels, but it isn't the kind of modest hostel or foyer that acts as a shorthand for poverty, either.

This hotel shapes and scaffolds the narrative of *I Can't Sleep*. First, it catalyzes social relationships between strangers, encouraging the kind of unbidden intimacies that are fodder for the cinema. When we stay in a hotel, we never know exactly who might be sleeping next door to us. When resident-chambermaid Daïga cleans Camille's room, she chances upon a series of black-and-white photographs that reveal his second life as a cabaret dancer in a drag bar. She then finds a suitcase of cash that points, obliquely, to another aspect of his double life. While the picture she paints of him is necessarily partial, every item discarded in a hotel garbage can or strewn on the floor can tell a story. If "hotels throw strangers together in chance arrangements," as Koestenbaum writes, then perhaps it is little surprise that these dwelling spaces have often played a crucial role in the dramatic arts.[4] Just consider the inns that populate the genre of the comedy of errors—spaces whose multiple adjoining rooms are ripe for enacting the transgressions, missteps, and social "errors" that lend the genre its name—or the flophouses that populate film noir. These buildings are particularly well suited to hosting multiplot stories in which separate narrative strands might first unravel in parallel before momentarily overlapping in a lobby or a stairwell.[5]

Second, the space of the hotel in Denis's film is also central to an exploration of labor relations. The patient camera of her cinematographer, Agnès Godard, attends to rhythms of manual labor: of Daïga tidying rooms, scrubbing washbasins, and—perhaps most memorably—vacuuming rooms with a cigarette in hand, much to the annoyance of her colleagues. By putting on display those forms of work that mainstream cinema habitually screens from view, we are enjoined to think about how it typically falls to those marked as "foreign."

Third, and relatedly, the hotel's lexical and symbolic association with hospitality brings into view a whole host of polemical questions that resonate with particular force in

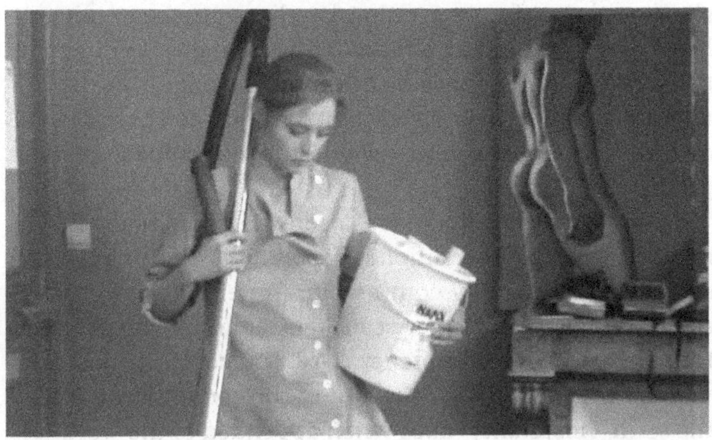

modern France and were a hot issue around the time of the film's release. In 1995 philosopher Jacques Derrida published an essay, one of his most influential, on the subject of hospitality. In it, he discusses the "troubling origins" of the term, whose Latin root—*hospis*—also yields the term "hostility," signaling a critical tension at the very heart of the word's etymology.[6] Derrida goes on to diagram a tension between what he calls an ethics of hospitality (the imperative to unconditionally welcome the stranger into one's house) and a politics of hospitality (welcoming the stranger within a context of finite resources, and with strings attached). The reconciliation of these tensions was crucially important in the context of greater European integration in the early 1990s, of course, as nation-states were redrawing their boundaries and navigating the threshold of inclusion and exclusion. By cataloguing the indignities and microaggressions that shape the everyday existence of "foreign" subjects, *I Can't Sleep* offers a sharp critique of a France that is reliant on cheap migrant labor to sustain its hospitality industry and to be "open to the world." And by choosing to center the plights of the immigrant chambermaid, Daïga, and the maligned postcolonial avatar, Camille, the film reveals the hollowness of that promise.

Is the "hospitality industry" a contradiction in terms? We may wonder. Can "conditional hospitality," a form of generosity underpinned by commercial imperatives, ever truly exist? A recent dialogue between French philosopher Gabrielle Halpern and Parisian hotelier Cyril Aouizerate provides us with a theoretically rich account of the semantic work that the term "hospitality" does when appended to the word "industry." For them, the hotel is an ambivalent space that acts both as wider society's "mirror" and its "blind spot," "reflecting societal needs, habits, prejudices, anxieties, and fantasies."[7] Little wonder, then, that Denis—a filmmaker with a sustained commitment to questions of borders, otherness, and foreignness—often turns to the hotel into a privileged space for exploring guest/host and self/other relations across a range of scales, both affective and geopolitical.

* * *

Cinema plays an important though curiously overlooked role in shaping and sustaining the tourist imaginary. The medium makes vicarious travelers of its spectators, fueling our desire to know and encounter the world. And to be a little more literal: film-induced tourism is a rapidly growing industry that shows little sign of abating. But what happens when the cinephile's expectations do not meet the tourist's reality? What happens when the passage from "reel" to "real" is experienced as an intense disappointment? There is a name for this phenomenon: Paris syndrome. This toponym describes the disorienting effects that occur when the reality of a place does not meet one's prior expectations—expectations, it is worth saying, that are often influenced by cinema.

I have always been struck by Claire Denis's attempt to capture something of the *real* Paris. As a former resident of the neighborhood in which *I Can't Sleep* is set, I recognize something of its feel. The film provides an antidote to the kind of saccharine, whitewashed view of Paris, and Montmartre in particular, that circulates in popular culture and would later be emblematized in a film like Jean-Paul Jeunet's *Amélie* (2001). As film critic Serge Kaganski describes, the Paris of *Amélie* is akin to the snow globes that crowd the shopfronts of present-day Montmartre. Jeunet's rendering of the city, he continues, is "meticulously cleansed of its ethnic, social, sexual and cultural polysemy."[8]

Yet, in the face of that film's eponymous heroine—the doe-eyed Amélie Poulain, played by Audrey Tautou—I also catch a faint glimpse of another character, one the actress would play in the subsequent year. In Stephen Frears's *Dirty Pretty Things* (2002), Tautou is no longer a poster girl for a troublingly untroubled vision of innocent whiteness, but rather an economic migrant living a clandestine existence in early 2000s London. Here she plays Senay, a Muslim Turkish cleaner at the luxury Baltic Hotel in Westminster, who works alongside Okwe, an undocumented migrant of Nigerian origin. In a twist that brings us unexpectedly much closer to the thematic terrain of a slightly later Denis film, *The Intruder* (2004), the two characters find themselves at the heart of an elaborate organ trafficking operation that involves their own bodies and those of unsuspecting hotel guests. The final, grim task of Senay's unregulated kidney transplant is undertaken in the ultimate hope of securing passports and a future free from the imminent threat of deportation.

Frears's thriller—which, like its film noir antecedents, depicts the hotel as a seedy hotbed of transactionality and criminality—brings a very different aspect of the relationship between cinema and the hotel squarely into view: the long association between hotels and the transgression of private space. The hotel industry is reliant on trust and anxieties are allayed by money. The contract seems self-evident: by placing our credit card into the hands of hotel staff we are placing ourselves in the hands of strangers who will show us to rooms in which might sleep, shower, have sex, or generally be at our most vulnerable. We hope never to learn the flimsiness of a cardboard "Do Not Disturb" sign the hard way, let alone that of Marion Crane's translucent shower curtain.[9] By positing a connection between the disappearance of bodies in the hotel and the invisibilized body of the migrant worker, *Dirty Pretty Things* provocatively invites us to consider what these logics of (in)visibility might have in common, pointing to a criminal netherworld most guests never see.

* * *

In spite of the ubiquity of hotel spaces in cinema, and the film industry's reliance on the hospitality industry, the relation between these two realms is rarely the topic of sustained reflection. In "Clean Architecture in Danger," German critic Frieda Grafe notes that in the early twentieth century "film festivals came into being to fill the empty beds in seaside resorts when they lay dormant, in the hors saison."[10] And the films screened at such events would themselves broadcast images of the latest, most desirable hotel spaces, acting as part of the hotel's promotional apparatus. This led to a cozy relationship that "went back and forth" throughout the years, constantly shifting in response to an ever-changing media—and tourist—landscape.

In 1920s Germany, the "Hotelfilm" was a short-lived film genre that was popularized by the UFA movie studio, counting F. W. Murnau's *The Last Laugh* (*Der letzte mann*, 1924) among its most popular examples. Grafe describes a similar genre in postwar Italy that was shaped in part by the fact that one of Italy's most influential producers of the 1950s and 1960s, Angelo Rizzoni, was also a hotel magnate.[11] Cinema, it turns out, has a long history of getting into bed with the hotel industry. But lest we assume that such opportunism would yield only substandard work, the partnership would lead to such films as Federico Fellini's *8½* (*Otto e mezzo*, 1963), an audacious and intensely self-referential film about the process of making a film. *8½* takes place across several hotels and spa resorts—its most memorable backdrop is perhaps the Grand Hotel La Fonte, in Anzio, a seaside harbor town south of Rome. Marcello Mastroianni plays Guido Anselmi, a thinly veiled stand-in for Fellini himself, who undertakes the tortuous process of creating a film from scratch. The embattled production process of the film-within-a-film resonates with the deep-seated existential angst that consumes the director. Vacant hotel spaces are used to great expressive potential; through the use of low-angle camera shots, the immense scale of the grand hotels dwarfs the human bodies that inhabit them, as does the scaffolding of film sets against which bodies also often appear. *8½* alerts us to the obvious fact that cinema is often conceived and produced while directors, actors, and industry professionals are housed in hotels. (In their 1991 film, *Barton Fink*, the Coen Brothers would add an important qualification: hotels are also spaces where film-scripts go to die.)

The relationship between the hotel and the cinema continues to evolve to this day, and in ways that Grafe's 1990 essay did not, and could not, anticipate. In early 2021 I increasingly noticed lifestyle publications such as *Condé Nast Traveler* and *Good Housekeeping* advertising "30 famous hotels from films you can actually stay in" and other such listicles. Most likely this can be attributed to the "frequency illusion," where one's bias toward some recently discovered idea renders it ubiquitous, but the timing of these editorials still somehow felt deliberate. Given that the coronavirus pandemic had put a halt to tourism and that at-home film and television services profited from their newly captive audiences, then what better way to ease tourists back into the world of travel than with safe and sanitized hotel rooms and the comfort of one's preexisting frame of cinematic reference?

For a hospitality industry that had been decimated by the pandemic, cinema would once again prove vital in rescuing its dwindling fortunes. The difficult year of 2021 also saw the opening of the Hotel Paradiso in Paris, which boasts the title of the world's first-ever "cinema-hotel." While on-demand viewing has constituted a key part of hotel experience for years, it had been a marginal aspect of tourism: it was part of the trip, but not the destination. Yet the Hotel Paradiso, conceived by the French cinema exhibitor and distributor mk2, billed itself as "a place where, for the first time, cinema is everywhere: in the traditional theatres, in the privacy of our rooms and suites transformed into screening spaces, and even on our rooftop terrain with its open-air cinema."[12]

Skeptical of these claims, and at a loss for what to do in eastern Paris one afternoon, I snuck into the establishment not long after its opening. The key, of course, is confidence. I wandered through corridors lined with DVD cases and dimly lit by red lights reminiscent of those found in recording studios. Walls were adorned with vintage posters, and a collaged image of Charlie Chaplin peeped out from the wall located in the building's inner courtyard. I was particularly struck by how the Hotel Paradiso exhibits both a deference toward the past "classics" of cinema and a proprietary insistence on its own novelty (oft-repeated claims to be the "first ever cinema-hotel") that feels entirely consonant with the conservative, outmoded understandings of cinephilia that scholars and critics are increasingly calling into question. If the hotel's creators had looked beyond this limited frame of reference, they might have noticed that such claims fail to stack up.

For instance, in January 2018, a few years prior to the opening of the Paradiso, Thai filmmaker Apichatpong Weerasethakul created an experimental living work of art, known as *SLEEPCINEMAHOTEL*, as part of Rotterdam's International Film Festival. This was an immersive cinema experience housed in the Zaal Staal, an event space in the Postillion Convention Centre. It consisted of single and double beds, built into a scaffolded structure, as well as a large circular screen on a central wall showing fragments from films that Apichatpong had gleaned from the archives of Amsterdam's EYE Filmmuseum. While the shape of the screen played with ideas of the hotel room peephole, magnifying images of a world outside, the architectural distinction between the inside and outside space of the hotel room started to slacken; while canopy-like canvases acted as translucent shelters, allowing guests of the cinema-hotel some privacy, and dim lanterns offered them their own source of light, the arrangement of architectural elements models an ethos of communal togetherness. Another part of the installation was open throughout the day; visitors who were not sleeping at the hotel were afforded a glimpse of Apichatpong's architecture from the vantage point of a balcony.

For Elena Gorfinkel, who experienced the ephemeral artwork firsthand, the temporary space that Apichatpong created recalls Roland Barthes's memorable analogy between filmgoers and silkworms in his 1975 essay "Leaving the Movie Theater." The space of the theatre becomes a "veritable cinematographic cocoon," encouraging a range of affective states and bodily comportments, tending toward slumber.[13] Another figure of thought from Barthes also comes to mind here. In a series of posthumously published lectures from 1977, Barthes mined a range of cultural texts and "novelistic spaces" that, he argued, offered inventive and compelling responses to the perennial question of "how to live together."[14] Living together, he argues, is not only a question of the shared occupation of space but also a question of time. He offers up the term *idiorrythmia* to describe the interplay between two forms of being, solitariness and association, whose alternating rhythms give meaning and texture to a shared social existence.

In "Leaving the Movie Theater," Barthes writes against the grain of dominant (abstract, idealist, disembodied) modes of thinking about spectatorship that circulated in the 1970s: a theater uncomplicated by the inconvenience of others, by the contagious joy of collective laughter, the frustrations of rustling popcorn, the very "stuff" of spectatorship.[15] For Barthes, entering the movie theatre was an exercise in how to live together. Apichatpong's participative project was also co-constituted by its guest-spectators: the artwork was shaped as much by the affective cadences of watching and sleeping, of being together and apart, as by any physical structure. By severing cinema's enchainment to narrative advancement (the visual track focused on images of bucolic landscapes, atmospheric skyscapes, and bodies of water) and by inviting overnight guests to extend the duration of their cinematic encounter (check-in opened at 4:00 pm, check out was at noon), *SLEEPCINEMAHOTEL* radically reimagined the spectatorial encounter. Apichatpong sought to induce a hypnagogic state in his guest-spectators, encouraging them to experience filmgoing on a slippery continuum from spectatorial alertness through to drift and into reverie. Rather than circulate in the realm of privatized experience, such as at the Hotel Paradiso, cinematic images were here a source of collective wonder and a catalyst of social interaction. Apichatpong's oneiric project returned to the hotel an idealized vision of hospitality premised on openness, communality, and association without guarantee.

Both the hotel and the cinema allow us to temporarily inhabit a time and space that is not our own; for a fee they offer an escape from the humdrum of our daily existence. In *Spectacle of Property* Rhodes advances a compelling hypothesis: "In purchasing a movie ticket spectator-tenants pay for the right to occupy a space in order to gaze up at a space they can never occupy."[16] As spectators encounter domestic space on film, they dwell in its architecture, coveting domestic goods and interior decor. The "spectacle" of property is a vehicle for advancing a promise of ownership, of spatial mastery, that is ultimately intangible and illusory. I have often wondered how substituting "house" for "hotel" here might push this suggestive analogy in a different direction. For a start, the abbreviated timeframe of hotel occupancy more closely resembles the time we take when watching a film (and this is especially the case with the condensation of time and space in the capsule hotel). And given that hotel architects are in the business of framing outdoor spaces and trading in exclusive window views, this suggests another point of similarity with the expropriative medium of film. The hotel and the cinema also share a certain performative dimension; both rely on artifice. This can be seen on a number of levels, ranging from the trivial (e.g., the books found on film sets and those that line the shelves of oak-paneled reading rooms of upscale hotels often share an ontological condition: they are fake) through to the more significant (e.g., the work of the front-of-house staff in a hotel is a kind of acting that might be described as affective labor).

* * *

Frieda Grafe describes the grand hotels that cropped up toward the end of the nineteenth century and proliferated on the screens of classical cinema as "a cinematographic topos, perhaps an allegory of cinema, or at least the cinema of a certain era."[17] And so while the historically contingent genre of the "hotel film" (in either its German or Italian iteration) had a short shelf life, the grand hotel seems to tell us something about modernity writ large.

Consider the opening scene of Edmund Goulding's *Grand Hotel* (1932). Well before the penniless baron (John Barrymore), dying accountant (Lionel Barrymore), Russian ballerina (Greta Garbo), and lowly stenographer (Joan Crawford) have appeared, the first shot pans above a series of female telephone operators at their switchboards. They are manually connecting calls, tapping away at buttons. The flurry of fast-paced hand gestures is accompanied by a babble of voices—variations on "Hello, Grand Hotel" delivered in clipped transatlantic accents. A dissolve brings us to the telephone booth in the lobby, where we witness fragments of conversations. These opening shots have little to impart other than a general impression of the 1920s hotel lobby as the social network of its age, a hub for hubbub. (As one veteran hotel resident memorably—and presciently—puts it: "People coming, going. Nothing ever happens.")

Goulding's interest lies in depicting the hotel as a medium that forges connections between people. The cinema feels uniquely well placed to capture this vision. The possibility of making contact—via telephone wires, in the elevator, or the lobby—entails the risk of missing connections or getting one's wires crossed. If the links between modernity, cinema, and the hotel are not explicit enough, the film cuts to an aerial shot of the reception lobby (captured from the vantage point of the hotel's circular atrium), which strikingly resembles the shape of a camera lens. Goulding's film is, perhaps above all else, one that spectacularizes the relationship between a dominant mode of cinema—classical Hollywood film—and a genre of hotels that similarly enjoyed a cultural hegemony at the time: the eponymous "grand hotels" of yesteryear.

These two media forms are knotted together like a Möbius strip, so that it becomes difficult to get a critical purchase on either term independently of the other. As we peer down through the hotel's circular atrium, which bears a structural resonance with the aperture of the camera, we feel the weight

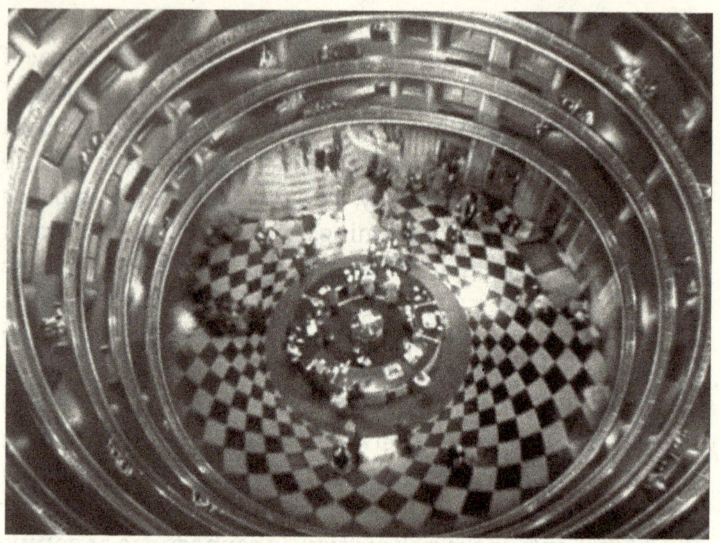

of our gaze dragged downward in a vertiginous, spiraling gesture.

Such entwinements of cinema and the hotel are this book's subject. The following chapters explore how filmmakers engage with a variety of hotel spaces, and, in a reverse gesture, the ways in which the hospitality industry folds cinema into its own cultural offering. In so doing, this book invokes the thinking of a range of cultural and critical theorists of space, whose own interests in the hotel (whether apprehended as physical space or approached as symbolic form) I want to briefly mention in closing.

Edmund Goulding's bold imagining of the hotel lobby as a stage upon which the dynamics of modernity are played out finds a point of consonance with the writing of Siegfried

Kracauer, for whom such lobbies represent a "gateway to the metropolis" (thereby fulfilling a symbolic role not dissimilar to the passageway for Walter Benjamin).[18] The hotel lobby, as Kracauer envisages it, is also a privileged ground for new (modern, secular) forms of sociality and communion. In drawing attention to the hotel as a rich locus of social inquiry, he is far from alone. For fellow Frankfurt School theorist Theodor Adorno—who in one of *Minima Moralia*'s more prickly passages treats his readers to a meditation on "chilly hospitality"—the hotel assumes a metonymic function, representing a loss of civility and proper service in an age increasingly governed by "automatized services," cost-cutting measures, and a poorly conceived division of labor.[19] The take of another cultural outsider, Henry James, is by contrast a little warmer; the "hotel-spirit" or "hotel civilization" represents for him a distinctively American attachment to comfort and convenience.[20] Beyond this modernist frame, too, the hotel resonates for thinkers such as Fredric Jameson, who famously invoked the example of Los Angeles's Westin Bonaventure to illustrate his account not just of what postmodernism is but also *how it feels*.[21] Much like the multifunctional spaces of its ballrooms or its suites, the hotel's meanings and philosophical valences can be rearranged, reorganized, and inhabited in different ways. As such, this book is not beholden to any particular "theory" of the hotel; rather, it undertakes a more speculative exercise in seeing how contrasting and conflicting modes of thought might temporarily cohabit under a shared roof. By apprehending this space through the prism of cinema (whether modern, postmodern, or otherwise) my interest lies in treating the hotel as a narrative tool, a way of structuring space, time, and social relations.

A key reason why the hotel so captures the attention of filmmakers, spatial theorists, and cultural critics, I wager, is precisely because these sites of temporary dwelling are caught in between the binary distinctions that we use to make sense of our environments and, by extension, the place we occupy in the world. Hotel encounters entail a rethinking of relationship between home and nonhome, public and private, intimacy and impersonality, labor and leisure, and the local and global. Focusing (on) the camera's aperture as one of these critical lenses, the following essays think through the cinematic hotel as a spatial medium, a narrative scaffold, and a rich historical archive.

2

Labor, Leisure, and Visual Pleasure

F. W. Murnau's silent expressionist film *Der letzte Mann/The Last Laugh* (1924), tells the story of an aging hotel porter (Emil Jannings) who works at the upmarket Atlantic Hotel in Berlin. The porter goes into work one morning to learn that he has lost his job because a manager witnessed him taking a rest in the lobby the previous day. He is promptly stripped of his elaborate uniform, a relic from a bygone imperial era, and demoted to the lowly role of washroom attendant. Although he continues to wear his uniform to and from work to disguise this change of status, word quickly gets out. Upon his return to his apartment block one evening, his neighbors greet him with ridicule. This represents just one of the indignities the ex-porter is made to endure. In a hallucinatory sequence that captures this moment, Murnau combines by way of superimposition a medium-long shot of the residents mocking him as they peer out of their windows and close-ups of an old laughing woman. Her ghostly face, dwarfing

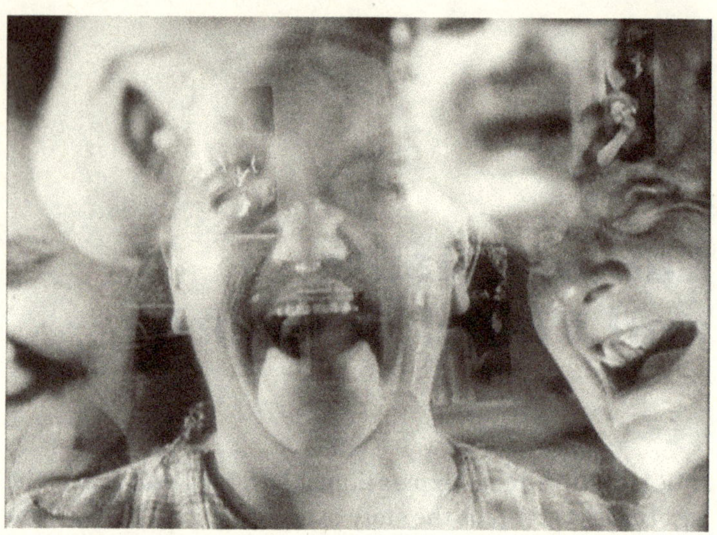

the crowd in the background, is simultaneously presented from multiple angles to generate a dizzying kaleidoscopic effect.

Just as the clientele of the hotel come and go, so too does its staff. Indeed, the revolving door—which helps to stage our own point of entry into the film—serves as an apt metaphor for the fungibility and expropriability of labor that is at stake in *The Last Laugh.*[1] Murnau's drab film offers a pathos-laden critique of working relations. As it reaches its dramatic crescendo, we watch the feeble, aging protagonist tucked up in the hotel bathroom with only a blanket to stave off the cold. However, in a dramatic reversal of fortunes, the scene is followed by an unusual intertitle: "Here our story should really end, for in actual life the forlorn old man would have little to look forward to but death. The author took pity on him, however, and provided quite an improbable epilogue." The film reveals the ex-porter to be the sole beneficiary of the will left by a wealthy patron of the hotel, whose deeds stipulate that his fortune should go to whomever is currently working as washroom attendant. In the final scene, we watch Jannings's character patronizing the very same hotel in which he worked for years. He indulges in copious meals with champagne and caviar and invites his colleagues to enjoy the bounteous fruits of his good fortune.

"Here our story *should really* end." The subtext of Murnau's intertitle comes more clearly into view if we dig into the checkered production history of *The Last Laugh*. The film's deus-ex-machina resolution was not, in fact, a product of authorial intervention, as the intertitle suggests. Rather, according to Murnau, it was imposed by UFA in order to lighten the film's mood and ensure its commercial viability.[2] Not only is the porter subject to the disciplinary gaze of the stern hotel manager, then, but he is also subservient to the wishes of the film's producers and imagined audience members who, we are told, would not want to see the grim implications of such punishment through to the end. Despite the film's putative happy ending—one that allows Jannings's character to clock out as a worker and check in as a patron—he is ultimately unable to escape his service role.

This example neatly illustrates an important dimension of labor in the hospitality industry: its performative aspect. In hotels, client-facing roles involve the performative demands of affective labor. It is necessary for workers to modulate their affective disposition to placate the guilt experienced by the onlooking guest-spectator.

Cinema and hotels: both are more commonly associated with the realm of leisure rather than that of labor. This is for good reason, given that the promise of relaxation is key to their enduring commercial appeal. Yet this very same appeal is reliant on successfully concealing the arduous work that transpires behind the scenes. The cause-for-firing offense committed by the protagonist of *The Last Laugh* was to display the toil of his labor in the wrong place: the hotel lobby, in full view of its guests. Murnau's error was to belabor the bitter implications of this episode in the wrong place: commercial cinema.

The problem of hotel work's visibility is one that often leaves those lower down in the pecking order in a difficult position. On the one hand, bellboys and chambermaids toil under the watchful eye of the managerial class, who seek visual assurance that their subordinates are busy at work. Yet, on the other hand, this cadre of workers must also share space with guests who have paid a premium to temporarily inhabit a space where they are not reminded of work.

What happens when these two demands come into direct conflict? Service workers often land in hot water—literally so in the case of Alicia, a junior crewmember who works aboard a luxury yacht in Ruben Östlund's *Triangle of Sadness* (2021). In one scene a champagne-sipping heiress instructs the crewmember to "loosen up" and get in the jacuzzi. "I command you to enjoy the moment," she states imperiously, betraying just a hint of an understanding of the unequal power dynamics. Alicia's panic-stricken face suggests that she is feeling the sharp edge of the film's triangulation of power. Caught between an inability to say no to VIP guests and the strict prohibition against fraternizing with them, she tarries between the two conflicting demands. She smiles hesitantly, attempting to voice a polite but affirmative "no," but trips over her words. Vacillating, she is caught in a spider's web of double negatives. Finally she acquiesces to the guest's self-indulgent demands. While the aim of the scene is to provide a moment of levity, one with only the faintest whiff of sexual impropriety, the interaction leaves a bitter aftertaste. For while Östlund's films have been routinely praised for their timeliness, exhibiting what Georgie Carr terms a "flair for zeitgeisty political engagement," the exploration of class relations in *Triangle of Sadness* steers largely clear of the more discomfiting aspects of these asymmetries of power,[3] especially for young women working in a service economy in which the words "yes" and "no" seem to have lost some of their fixity. Given that the hotel, or in this case the luxury yacht, contains a complex admixture of work and play, the thin line between these spheres is often strategically manipulated to emphasize a loose continuum between different forms of gendered service work, from housekeeping to childcare to sex work.

* * *

Before the start of his filmmaking career in the early 1980s, Atom Egoyan worked for five years sorting and cleaning linen at the Empress Hotel in Victoria, British Columbia. While this job was a means to an end, Egoyan has spoken in detail about how it shaped his approach to filmmaking: "Both professions involve the creation of illusion," he explains in a short essay reflecting on his film practice.[4] Elsewhere, Egoyan has spoken of being "fascinated by the process of preparing a room for someone to come into, so that the guest would believe it was virgin territory."[5] The suggestive parallels between hotel work and cinematic labor that Egoyan has discussed on many occasions are pursued further in his early film *Speaking Parts* (1989).

Set in Toronto's upmarket Windsor Arms hotel, *Speaking Parts* explores the interwoven trajectories of three characters. First we are introduced to a screenwriter named Clara, a guest at the hotel. She develops a filmscript in order to work through her attachment to her recently deceased brother, Clarence, whose grainy image we see in the opening scene and whose phantom presence casts a penumbral shadow over the film. Clara becomes intimately involved with Lance, a housekeeper who strongly resembles her brother. In addition to his day job, Lance moonlights as a bit-part actor and services hotel guests in his third job as an escort. He is the object of intense fixation for the film's third central character, Lisa, a fellow housekeeper. Lisa spends her evenings poring over Lance's varied filmography. She consumes his films with voracious insistence, periodically stilling the moving images that contain fleeting glimpses of Lance's presence. If this synopsis invites confusion, not least because of the similar names of characters—Clara, Clarence, Lance, Lisa—and the weakness of the ties that bind them, then this is, in a sense, the film's point. Egoyan asks us to consider what happens when our desires for lost objects become reinvested in new bodies; *Speaking Parts* is about desire's shapeshifting quality, its mutability, its deterritorialization. Indeed, the space of the hotel seems to accentuate and facilitate these particular qualities of desire given that their patrons are brought out of their domestic—and erotically domesticated—contexts and drawn into intimate proximity with other strangers.

Both women's fixation on Lance is mediated by cinema. In keeping with the postmodern idiom of the film, their fascination is ultimately a fascination with his image. We watch the screen tests that Lance undertakes for Clara from the small screen of a handheld video recorder; we see grainy shots of VHS images up close, catalyzing the kind of tactile eroticism that remains beyond Lisa's grasp for most of the film. And in early scenes that focus on Lance at work—scrubbing the bathroom, smoothing starched white sheets—we, too, are invited to linger on his body. The banality of the manual work coupled with his dedramatized acting style render this bodily presence even more conspicuous. Scenes of cleaning toilets and making beds are suffused with a surprisingly erotic tension.

While the conspicuousness of the film's style, high postmodernism with a baroque flourish, resists any easy absorption into a broader genre of films, *Speaking Parts* shares much common ground with *I Can't Sleep*.[6] Much like Claire Denis, Egoyan exploits the narrative possibilities of the spatial threshold; the labyrinthine architecture of the hotel helps him to gradually stage multiple points of entry into the elaborate and elliptical social fabric of the film, though this will be fully revealed only by the film's end. And in spite of their myriad differences, his characters are similarly ground in a shared sense of groundlessness, restlessness, drift, and despondency. But while Denis's protagonist, Daïga, saw a male director's invitation to abandon her job as a chambermaid for the glamorous world of acting for what it was (namely, a hollow promise and a bid to gain sexual intimacy), Lance chooses a different path.

Speaking Parts has typically been read as a film about unrequited love, psychic transference, and the consumption of images in a postmodern mediascape. It was even the privileged object of a philosophical disagreement between Jean Baudrillard and Paul Virilio.[7] While it may well be all of those things, it is also a story about work. More pointedly, the film investigates various, often overlapping, forms of work—cleaning, hospitality, performance labor, sex work—and the narrowing space between them when the culture industry and the hospitality industry come into intimate contact.

In an early scene we observe Lance cleaning Clara's room. He chances upon a draft of her filmscript lying on her bedroom dresser. He decides to slip his casting card under her door, which secures him an audition. By offering his body to Clara after the audition, Lance sees an opportunity to become more than an extra, a human prop, a nameless character on screen. Sexual intimacy is what will seal the deal for the much coveted "speaking part" in Clara's film, and with it the hope of career advancement. The title of Egoyan's film refers to the size of film roles and the value (symbolic and economic) ascribed to different kinds of performance labor. In the film industry, characters with narrative significance are most likely those who speak, whereas nonspeaking parts typically assume a minor role and commonly recede into the background. A similar principle is also at play in the hotel industry, where "speaking parts" (front-of-house or client-facing roles) are imputed greater value than nonspeaking parts, such as housekeepers or kitchen staff, who are often drawn from immigrant communities where English (assuming this is the lingua franca) is rarely a worker's first language. In the dual contexts of performance labor and hotel work, then, speech is given to those who are granted personhood, those whose capacities for intersubjective relations are deemed valuable.

Egoyan throws into the mix a third form of labor—sex work—which complicates the relationship between speech and the body. For while anti–sex work rhetoric has traditionally focused on the status of the body in sex work by calling attention to the harms associated with reducing persons to bodies, its advocates also foreground the body in order to desensationalize sex work, situating it in proximity to other forms of embodied labor and care work (or what sociologist Carol Wolkowitz terms "body work").[8] As with the field of acting, in sex work speech plays an important role in the management of intimacy, the authentication of bodily pleasure, and the "ratification" of sexual gratification.

Speaking Parts frequently cuts between scenes of screen acting, sex work, and hotel labor, inviting us to consider the relationship between them. For instance, in an early scene in a video rental store Lisa is quizzed by the manager about her rental history, which seems, in generic terms at least, to have little consistency. The answer, of course, is that all these films feature appearances by Lance. "Well, he may be in these movies, but he doesn't have a speaking part," the video clerk notes, to which Lisa answers, "but there's nothing special about words." We then cut to a scene, which is already mid-conversation, in which the hotel's head housekeeper conducts a performance review with Lance. "And then there are those that complain that you're not vocal enough," she says, referring not to his cleaning role but to the sex work that she will schedule for him. The parallels here are striking enough: sex work figures as a direct continuation of Lance's work as an actor and as a cleaner. Over the course of their conversation, his boss assumes a variety of roles: line manager, talent agent, intimacy coordinator, and pimp.

In her account of the relationship between labor and performance in cinema, Elena Gorfinkel understands onscreen acting as a form of immaterial labor. She draws attention to how the cinematic apparatus captures the performing body and, in a gesture of expropriation, extracts from the body at work an image to be consumed: "Alienated from the product of their labor as well as from their audience in ways that are fundamental to the nature of cinematic production, circulation, and exhibition, the screen performers' physical presence is expropriated and refigured: reedited, reframed, and retemporalized."[9]

Drawing attention to the circulation of screen-based technologies, Egoyan is also interested in such gestures of expropriation, especially when they involve both sex and power. When placed in Lisa's hands, for instance, Lance's bit-parts become media objects to be played with and indeed reframed and retemporalized with the ritual insistence of a fetishist. Egoyan, like Gorfinkel, is also careful to counterbalance this attention to the immateriality of cinematic images with a thoroughly *materialist* exploration of the conditions in which cinema is made. *Speaking Parts* alerts us to how the hotel and the multiple forms of labor that transpire within it play a crucial role in cinema's broader networks of production. Following the screen test, Lance and Clara have sex in her hotel suite. The morning after, the sheets will be stripped from the bed to maintain what Egoyan earlier described as the illusion of "virgin territory." Presumably they will be sent down the laundry chute to be processed by Lisa, who will remain unaware of her proximity to Lance's body.

If the medium of cinema tends to consign the materiality of labor offscreen, then the hotel's laundry chute serves a similar role of the management of materiality, waste, and the stubborn residues of daily life. And while we would be hard pressed to read *Speaking Parts* as a metacritical exposition of the film industry's own dirty laundry (it would be a mistake, in my mind, to reduce Egoyan's cinema to such simplistic didacticism), the film nonetheless invites us to reflect upon cinema's showing and concealing of the social processes that go into "the work of the image."

* * *

In her book on Egoyan, Emma Wilson describes the filmmaker's approach to the narrative space of the hotel as akin to a puzzle, a "nexus of meanings and connections" that we can only come to apprehend gradually, in the absence of a definitive floor plan or screenplay to consult in advance.[10] She also draws connections between Egoyan's piecemeal scattering of clues and details (the "material and photographic objects, video images" that help us to build a gradual view of the protagonists' "affective and mourning histories") and the approach to documenting hotel life that French conceptual artist Sophie Calle undertook in the early 1980s.

In 1981 Calle took a job as a chambermaid in a hotel in Venice to secure access to hotel rooms and to take pictures of personal effects that guests would leave behind during the day. The resultant photographs formed the basis for *The Hotel*, which includes images of unmade beds, unpacked suitcases, and full wastepaper bins, accompanied by a dry, observational written record of the state in which the rooms were found. Calle's project offered an inventory of intimate but anonymous details, the ephemeral traces of waste that are there in the morning but will be gone by the evening. By documenting the remnants of anonymous lives, Calle's aim was not necessarily to expose the dirty laundry of the Venice hotel's well-off patrons but rather to reveal the embarrassment of ethnographic riches that hide in plain sight for the covert chambermaid-cum-photographer. Both *Speaking Parts* and *The Hotel*, Wilson writes, offer an "archaeology of the present."[11] The question of labor that sustains Egoyan's attention, however, is conspicuously absent from Calle's project, which contains little by way of a reflection on class relations or political economy. We have to look elsewhere for a lens-based meditation on hotel work. Fortunately for us, however, a more recent text that emerged as a direct response to Calle's work, Lila Avilés's 2018 film, *La camerista/The Chambermaid*, tells a different story.

* * *

In the hotel room, the presence of the labor that has transpired in a guest's absence is largely effaced, save a few deliberately small details that might otherwise escape our attention. In a "turndown service," pillows are plumped and curtains drawn, generating the mise-en-scène of and the affective conditions for a guest's relaxation after a busy day. The exposed corners of toilet paper are tucked inward as if to mimic the form of an envelope, though the sender of the missive is meant to remain anonymous. Subtle cues like this function as indices that work has taken place, but they ought never to be conspicuous. A bad job will be visible to the guest's eye, whereas good work is self-effacing.

To creatively extend Egoyan's earlier musings: What might it mean to think of the mise-en-scène of the hotel room as somehow akin to the labor of cinematic production and editing? Or to think of the "touching up" of images as somehow analogous to a "turndown" service? Three things that this admittedly strained and tendentious line of questioning does have the merit of bringing into view are (1) that these forms of work constitute forms of aesthetic labor; (2) they both entail processes of negation; and (3), perhaps by virtue of the previous two points, such behind-the-scenes work has historically often fallen to women.

The aporia of labor's visibility is central to *The Chambermaid* given that Avilés's film foregrounds the world of work that the hospitality industry wants to hide. Set entirely in the spaces of the InterContinental Presidente in Mexico City, the film chronicles the daily life of Eve, a twenty-five-year-old woman who works as a chambermaid in the upscale hotel. As we patiently observe the quotidian rhythms of her work schedule, days quickly blur into one. Scenes of Eve cleaning are punctuated with a string of encounters with guests and colleagues: she strikes up a friendship with Minitoy, whom she meets in adult education classes; she briefly flirts with the window cleaner; she makes repeated inquiries about a red dress in her size that one of the guests abandoned. While Eve is forced to leave behind her personal life as she clocks into work, we come to learn that she lives with her son some two hours away, on the outskirts of town, in a neighborhood without running water. The sumptuous world of luxury hotels she enters on daily basis is worlds apart from her home life.[12] This personal sphere remains firmly off screen; we ascertain its details only via conversational fragments and one-sided telephone calls.

The film opens with a reflexive gesture that shows the "work" that goes into the mise-en-scène of the image. The first shot comes into view with the raising of an electric blind, which gradually reveals a close-up of Eve in a hotel room. We are far from the "virgin territory" of which Egoyan spoke. Rather, a medium shot presents an unmade room in a state of disarray. Eve starts tidying the objects strewn out on the bed and floor with military precision. A kettle starts to whistle. The camera remains static while she moves in and out of the tight frame. Avilés uses dorsal shots to frustrate our access to Eve's subjectivity and demands that we focus on her action. She pauses to sniff a towel on the bedroom floor, cleans the bathrooms, and uses bin bags to transport sodden bath towels. When making the bed she discovers the body of an old man, whom she first suspects to be a corpse. Unfazed, the guest at first refuses to acknowledge her presence before shooing Eve away with a dismissive gesture that sets the tone for the rest of the film's social interactions.

Many scenes will unfold in a similar way: we first observe Eve as she undertakes a cleaning duty with mathematical precision; we grow increasingly invested in the spectacle of her movements and gestures; the activity is disrupted when she finds some small detail (a camera, some photographs, or a book left on a counter) which prompts her to carve out a momentary space for curiosity, reverie, or respite from the otherwise unrelenting pace of her work. Although brief moments like these humanize the film's protagonist—setting her apart from Calle's detached, ethnographic mode of material observation—Eve's gentle, stoic, placid disposition also makes the challenges she routinely encounters even more painful to watch.

We learn that Eve is currently assigned to the twenty-first floor of the hotel but aspires to work in the penthouses on the forty-second floor. The neatness of these two numbers—the second of which is a multiple of the first—tells us something about the hollowness and arbitrariness of the hotel's approach to Eve's professional development. (Are we to expect that the forty-second floor is exactly twice as prestigious as the twenty-first?) What is certain is that within the imposing architecture of the hotel, verticality reigns supreme and everybody is supposed to know their place. In *Hotel Life*, Caroline Levander and Matthew Guterl write of how hotel architectures "dole out space and align it with socioeconomic privilege."[13] We would be hard-pressed to find a more striking exemplification of this logic than we do in the InterContinental Presidente.

By moving beyond a general critique of exploitative labor practices, Avilés shows us how access to the privileged spaces of the hotel is underwritten by a subtle set of racial and geopolitical tensions that are *intra*continental. On the second day Eve is summoned to the room of a wealthy Argentinian woman, Romi, who asks her to look after her baby while she takes a shower—a role that goes far beyond Eve's formal duties and strays into the terrain of care work. If the conflation of these roles ought to be understood within broader traditions, across Latin America, of indigenous domestic workers undertaking the dual roles of maid and nanny (a position memorably embodied by Cléo in Alfonso Cuarón's *Roma*), the subsequent conversation brings more squarely into view the subtle ways in which racism continues to operate in present day Mexico City. Romi, a white Argentinian woman, asks Eve, who is of indigenous Mexican descent, a series of racist questions about the customs of local women, ranging from their dietary choices to grooming habits. What is remarkable is not the content of Romi's chauvinism, which gives voice to a predictably racialized hierarchy among Latin American populations, but rather the formal composition of the shots and the visual backdrop against which these cross-cultural interactions take place. As she absorbs Romi's words, Eve casts her glance outward toward the plate-glass windows of the luxury suite, revealing breathtaking views down onto Mexico City—her city—below. Far from offering a sense of perceptual freedom for Eve, her gaze in this moment registers a sense of social displacement and spatial dispossession. As her interactions with Romi make abundantly clear, the enviable views in which the hotel trades are not intended for people like her.

Through the architectural arrangement of the InterContinental Presidente's luxury suites, which are made to the measure of the jet-setting international clientele rather than local working-class populations, the common space of the cityscape assumes the status of a private commodity. The hotel's most remarkable feature, its unrivaled window views, virtually extends the space of the room into the cityscape below, thus offering what Rhodes has called "a sense of proprietorship" for its intended guests, a "bringing close" and a "visual appropriation of a world that does not belong" to the occupant.[14] As his study goes on to remind us, these logics of visual and spatial appropriation are often made possible at the expense of dispossessing local, working-class populations. As the taciturn Eve gently rocks the baby stroller back and forth, glancing into the middle distance, her own gaze and bodily comportment register the effects of this expropriating gesture.

Avilés's film disabuses us of the neoliberal myth that social and professional advancement can be wrought solely by hard work and determination. *The Chambermaid* is a Sisyphean tale: no matter how hard Eve works, the elusive promise of a promotion lays out of her grasp. But Avilés is perhaps less interested in exposing the mechanisms of the "glass ceiling," in which an unacknowledged barrier creates an obstacle to professional advancement, than she is reflecting on glass windows. In the film, glass windows represent something of a ruse; they present a sense of freedom, opportunity, and contact with the outside world which appears unfettered, open to all. However, such seemingly basic freedoms are withheld from Eve who spends her waking hours inside the hotel and does not have the luxury of time.

* * *

The window occupies a key role in Jacques Rancière's meditation on working-class life, *Proletarian Nights*. Offering a corrective to Marxist analyses that treat the working class as a homogeneous group, the French philosopher excavates fragments from personal archives of nineteenth-century workers that offer rare insights into their thoughts, dreams, and inner lives. In one of the book's key passages he recalls a tile layer named Gabriel Gauny, who temporarily lays downs his tools and describes the experience of gazing out of a window while working on a floor. He writes: "If the window opens out on a garden or commands a view of a picturesque horizon, he stops his arms a moment and glides in imagination toward the spacious view to enjoy it better than the possessors of the neighboring residences."[15] Windows, as Rancière suggests, invite us to reflect on how we relate to the world outside, to temporarily reimagine our position in the world. To link this to the broader philosophical project for which Rancière is best known, built environments are political insofar as they frame the parameters of the seeable and the sensible: they shape and circumscribe our aesthetic and political horizon of possibility. As Gabriel Rockhill notes of this passage, "when he gazes out of the window during his workday, [the worker] breaks with this dominant order; he creates a fissure within the system of determination by appropriating the privileged activity—spectatorship—of the aesthete."[16] Sometimes it is necessary to steal moments of time out of the working day to reflect on our position within the world and even motivate us to action.

Eve is someone who intuitively understands this. She too steals brief moments from the working day to gaze out the window, to cultivate curiosity, to elaborate—at however small a level—some sense of autonomy and aesthetic resistance. One of the risks of creating expansive vistas is that it might lead workers to seek new horizons beyond work. In the final scenes of *The Chambermaid*, when she has learned of the unsuccessful outcome of her application for promotion, Eve takes her dress, heads up to the forty-second floor and its helicopter pad to survey the panoramic vista that was previously inaccessible to her. The final scene shows her leaving her place of work definitively and defiantly. Though viewers are under no illusion that her actions will lead to structural change (especially considering the principle of the revolving door that characterizes the hotel's approach to human resources), her gesture of resistance registers her muted wishes. As her friend and colleague Minitoy notes poignantly, "You're small, but you're strong."

The figure of the chambermaid, Salomé Aguilera Skvirsky has recently shown, is a powerful allegorical figure within Latin American cinema, not least because the origins of domestic service work return us to the history of colonialism.[17] While acknowledging this history in a specifically Mexican context and documenting the structural forces that produce the immiseration of workers, Avilés offers a sensitive portrait of the affective contours of a worker's subjectivity that is not simply reducible to the metonymic function that "the worker," as an all-encompassing allegorical category, is often made to embody. This is perhaps why the most memorable scene in the film (memorable, perhaps, by virtue of its inverse relation to the significance of the film as a whole) is one in which Eve carves out a thin slice of time, following her work break, to play. Although she subsists on a meager diet of popcorn, the cheapest item in the workplace canteen, Eve stashes away a little bit in her uniform along with stray scraps of paper, only to later fashion these into miniature popcorn bags when she is on her break. "Small, but strong," or strong by virtue of its smallness, the scene presents us with a window into Eve's rich imagination, transporting us momentarily beyond the restrictive workspace of the hotel and into a space of leisure.

* * *

For some working-class people, temporary lodgings are not only sites of work but also spaces of dwelling. To explore this often-overlooked aspect of precarious living it is necessary to enter the space of the *motel*, an altogether more modest setting that curbs some of the fanciful excesses associated with luxury accommodations. "Motel" is a portmanteau formed out of the contraction of "motor" and "hotel." Even at the level of language, functionality overrides aesthetic concerns: "motel" is a no-frills term that does exactly what it says on the tin. A similar principle of unfussiness governs the lodging type itself—stark and spartan, plain and functional, ordinary and impersonal. While prestige hotels act as "cultural conduits" for what Norman Klein has called a "cosmopolitan consciousness," the motel has little truck with such lofty ideals.[18]As the foremost theorist of this dwelling space, Bruno Bégout, suggests, they might best be described as "supermarkets of sleep."[19]

To my English ear, the word "motel" has an American twang to it. The genealogy of this dwelling space has a distinctly American history, too. In *Common Place: The American Motel*, Bégout notes that the earliest motels (which were commonly referred to as "auto courts" and "cabin camps") date back to the mid-1920s. The form grew in popularity in the postwar period. But just as the rising fortune of the motel can be indexed to the postwar economic boom in the United States, by the same token, the waning fortunes of the motel, and its changing cadre of occupants, are the result of the strains that the U.S. economy has faced in more recent decades. Bégout defines the motel as a transitory space where thrifty clients, drawn in by "the sole attraction of the low price," "stay one, maybe two nights."[20] Such a description fails, however, to capture the experiences of the growing number of Americans living paycheck to paycheck, for whom residency periods in motels far exceed the "one, maybe two nights" that owners and architects had originally envisaged.

The motel is a recurring location in *Nickel and Dimed* (2001), investigative journalist Barbara Ehrenreich's autoethnographic account of living on minimum wage in the United States in late 1990s.[21] Here the American institution plays a role that exceeds its originally intended purpose; it serves as a form of not-so-temporary accommodation for those shut out from a more traditional rental market. As Ehrenreich reminds us, motels are often the only viable form of accommodation for those living hand-to-mouth because its residents can pay the rent weekly rather than monthly, and there exist few of the barriers to entry that we associate with more traditional tenancy arrangements (hefty deposits, credit checks, legal screening, etc.). For these more casual lodging arrangements, which often require residents to move between motels every twenty-eight days to avoid gaining an entitlement to tenancy rights, occupants pay inflated rates relative to traditional housing. This represents just one aspect of the infamous "cost of being poor" that Ehrenreich so deftly outlines.

This phenomenon of not-so-temporary motel living is given dramatic form in Sean Baker's visually exuberant drama *The Florida Project* (2017), set in the Magic Castle Inn, a run-down motel in Kissimmee, just south of Orlando. The Magic Castle is one of a number of motels that were built off Highway 192 to cater to tourists making their way to and from Walt Disney World. In a bid to capture the passing trade and distinguish itself from its rival, the neighboring, aeronautically themed "Futureworld," the motel's facade is painted a lurid lilac and adorned with castle-like crenulations. The neighborhood in which the film is set was originally developed to evoke the whimsical world of Walt Disney. However, several factors, both global (the financial crash of 2008) and local (the rezoning of an extension of the Disney resort away from Osceola and into neighboring Orange County), conspired to turn Kissimmee into a ghost town. Amid the palm trees and vacant concrete parking lots, the streetscape is populated with dollar-store replicas of nearby attractions. While the town is haunted by the shadow of Walt Disney World, the price of the theme park's admission remains out of reach to many of its residents.

The Magic Castle Inn still retains its name for strategic purposes. Although the motel's manager, Bobby, earns his keep renting to the central Floridian precariat, the name is search-engine optimized to ensnare unsuspecting tourists without an eye to detail, who assume they have bagged a bargain within the safe hermetic enclosure of an official Walt Disney World lodging (the "Magic Kingdom") rather than what one duped Brazilian tourist dismissively calls "a slum, welfare motel." The film's titular "project" refers not only to the original 1960s code name for Disney's theme park, but also the motel's informal function as a social housing project. Every few days, a mobile food bank pitches up in the parking lot, around which the motel's architecture is organized, only to be asked by Bobby to go behind the building next time. The conspicuous signs of poverty risk breaking the Magic Castle's spell, not that many tourists would fall for its illusion.

Set over the course of a summer vacation, the story is told through the eyes of a precocious six-year-old, Moonee, who lives with her mom, Halley, in a single room on the third floor. Doling out lighthearted comedy and bruising pathos in equal measure, Baker's film alternates between scenes that present the vibrant social lives of unsupervised children, many of whom are nonprofessional actors, in a nod to an erstwhile cinematic tradition of neorealism, and scenes in which anxieties about how the mother-daughter duo will make rent weighs heavy on their minds. *The Florida Project* might seem

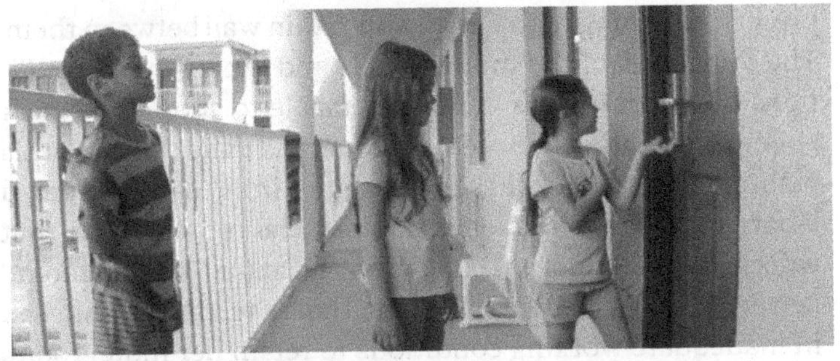

to have little to say about the question of work; Halley, after all, doesn't hold down a regular job, as her Social Security caseworker makes bluntly clear. But this surface description belies Baker's careful attention to a more informal economy of hustling and grifting. Moonee can lay her charm on thick as molasses when she needs to, guilting tourists into giving her money for ice cream. She and Halley spend their afternoons selling knock-off perfumes in the parking lots of neighboring country clubs. And, in a plot twist that we come to register only toward the end of the film, we learn that Halley also turns tricks to cobble together the rent. She receives johns in the family bed while Moonee takes a bubble bath in the en suite bathroom a few yards away. Rap music played on a phone speaker muffles the noise.

It is this last activity that will prompt the intervention of social workers, who pry the mother and daughter apart as the film ends. While there are clues that sex work is commonplace in the Magic Inn, the source of anxiety here stems from the fact that the spaces of work and play—two activities whose lines are already blurred throughout the film—take place in adjoining rooms with only a thin wall between them. The flimsiness of the motel's walls and the cramped conditions of working-class living are unable to shore up a clear spatial delineation between sex work and child's play. As this distinction starts to slacken, the film's interest in gendered labor gives way to anxieties about social reproduction that will cleave the "innocent child" away from the "welfare mom." Left with no viable work options, Halley resorts to paid sex in inadequate working conditions to retain her motel room. This same motel room, however, will compromise the very future that she and her daughter envisage. While very different from the patterns of poverty and structural inequality that Ehrenreich describes in her analysis of the Floridian precariat, both experiences of living are marked by a sense of circularity. Throughout much of the film, time is measured in twenty-eight-day cycles. (Up until the end of the film, that is, which ruptures this temporal loop and severs the maternal bond definitively.)

Given that Baker's film is set in the shadow of nearby Walt Disney World, we are asked to think about the relationship between capital, inequality, and the culture industry. What, after all, is the film if not an attempt to delaminate the picture postcard vision of Disney's Orlando that circulates in the popular imaginary? But while Disney tends to attract cultural criticism of a largely abstract variety (from Michael Sorkin's worry that visitors would be seduced by the simulacra to Baudrillard's claim that the unreality of Walt Disney World serves the structural function in shoring up the rest of America's sense of reality), Baker refuses the terms of these theoretically overheated debates.[22] His film is unwavering in its focus on, and commitment to, those who live on the theme park's margins; when it is not hewing to the body of Moonee and her friends his camera is attending to the junk, the debris, the material fallout from the immaterial fantasies that constitute the ideological ground on which Walt Disney's playland is built.

Midway through the film Moonee guides her friend Jancey, whose eyes she clasps shut, to the parking lot to witness a magical sight. She removes her hands, shouts "Open!," and points to the sky to reveal the rainbow, its arc stretching across the horizontal plane of the image. A fortuitous detail that occurred during the shooting of the film, one that Baker felt he had to seize upon, the rainbow's symbolism is obvious enough. It allegorizes the promise of a brighter world that lies just beyond the frame. (Or, to put this in slightly metaphysically contrived terms, it reveals the real-life fantasy realm that is tantalizingly close by.) The rainbow, of course, also represents an illusion, pointing to the necessary fictions that sustain the imaginations of these girls and the motel's residents before these notions turn, curdle, and fall prey to the logic of "cruel optimism," to invoke Lauren Berlant. In this bruising, poignant, and quietly devastating scene, my eye is not drawn to the rainbow and prepackaged symbolism that comes associate with it for very long. Rather, my gaze is swiftly drawn back to the spectacle of the motel, whose bold purple facade trumps any of the violet hues we might strain to discern at the rainbow's southernmost tip. Perhaps this is because the motel is so central to the film's narrative and its affective tone; the facade encapsulates the incommensurable gap between work and play, the visual exuberance of a fantasy world and the drab and dour reality of poverty and hardship. While the Magic Castle Inn is boldly imagined by Baker and his cast of nonprofessional actors as a playground, a thrilling place for wayward children to run free and play, it is also ultimately an example of when architecture just doesn't work.

* * *

"The cinema, in documentary and other forms, has rarely filmed work," writes Jean-Louis Comolli.[23] Grappling with a paradox that has mutely informed my discussion here, he leaves us with the suggestion that politically resistant film-making must somehow labor *against* the cinematic machine that so often renders work graceful, effortless, without heft, or absent entirely. In their various ways, the hotel films that we have encountered here have called these mechanisms into question, either by highlighting the burdens that hotels, as workplaces, place upon their employees or by drawing our eye to the antagonisms of labor that cinema habitually holds from view. The hotel, like the cinema, is an eminently *visual* medium, availing itself of spatial technologies (from the revolving doors to laundry chutes, from basement canteens to out-of-bounds bathrooms) to delimit the contours of labor's visibility, with clear political effects. In contravention of the "Do Not Disturb" signs hanging outside hotel room doors, the films explored here have each sought, in ways both big and small, to disturb the neat opposition between labor and leisure spaces upon which the organization of the hotel—and, following Comolli, *cinematic form*—so relies.

3

Lost in Space

In a discussion of Manhattan's Waldorf Astoria Hotel in *Delirious New York*, architect and urban theorist Rem Koolhaas makes a passing reference to cinema: "In the thirties—when the second Waldorf is being built—the 'Hotel' becomes Hollywood's favorite subject. In a sense, it relieves the scriptwriter of the obligation of inventing a plot. A Hotel is a plot—a cybernetic universe with its own laws generating random but fortuitous collisions between human beings who would never have met elsewhere."[1]

The broad shape of his argument is one that might now feel familiar to us, for what is the hotel if not a rich suggestive chronotope with which to scaffold a narrative? And what is the hotel good for, if not a ready-made "field for the comedy of clashing manners" from which scriptwriters can draw influence?[2] Yet as we read this passage a little more closely, at least two elements start to complicate this line of thinking. The first is Koolhaas's surprising invocation of cybernetics to name the virtual network of connections between bodies and spaces, which might strike the present-day reader as jarringly anachronistic when referring to the 1930s. Sure, we might explain Koolhaas's choice to superimpose this technical language onto an early twentieth-century moment in terms of the quirks of the object in question. The ever-changing space of Manhattan, after all, is one that seems to actively court palimpsestic readings. But in addition to the book's titular "delirium," Koolhaas's discussion of the Waldorf Astoria induces a kind of jet lag. It shuttles its readers across time zones and traces the affective pull of the past in the present, and vice versa.

Second, it is interesting to note the tension between collision, contingency, and the chaos of social interactions on the one hand and the organizing function of the hotel as a narrative container on the other. Koolhaas's formulation of setting-as-plot finds parallels in film theory. For instance, writing of apartments, Pamela Robertson Wojcik similarly encourages us to hear in the word "plot" a double meaning, referring both to a narrative structure and a space that is parceled off and destined to become real estate.[3]

While there are many cinematic examples in which hotel spaces are instrumentalized to drive forward a predetermined plot, we can also muster a corpus of cinematic counterexamples in which the hotel is a rich locus of narrative emptiness, meandering, and drift. A hotel is not always "a plot"; it can also be synonymous with plotlessness. This is precisely why Siegfried Kracauer likens the hotel lobby to a "negative church."[4] Unlike a church, in which the congregation waits for God, in the hotel lobby, which Kracauer envisages as an emblematic space of secular ritual, people wait for nothing.

Take *Last Year at Marienbad*, a 1960 collaboration between French filmmaker Alain Resnais and experimental writer Alain Robbe-Grillet. If there is one film that has come to exemplify the marriage between literary modernism's difficulty and midcentury art cinema's predilection for ambiguity (as well as serving as a scapegoat for their respective excesses), then *Marienbad* is surely it.[5] Set to the languid cadences of a pipe organ, the film takes place in a grand hotel somewhere in central Europe. The black-and-white cinematography and chiaroscuro lighting adds to its opulent aesthetic. The film's narrative form is equally baroque: it consists chiefly of recursive conversations between men and women that take place within a seemingly unending reserve of ballrooms.

After a while the film's iterative structure starts to fold in on itself, concertina-like. A man, "X" (Giorgio Albertazzi), approaches a woman, "A" (Delphine Seyrig), to say that he remembers their brief love affair the previous year. He maintains that she told him they should wait a year before they elope, but she has no recollection of the encounter. A second man (Sacha Pitoëff, perhaps A's husband) looks on. Though the film flirts with the trope of the multiplot hotel narrative and the elliptical scenes sow doubt, mystery, and intrigue, we soon grasp that our own detective work will be in vain.

What *Marienbad* lacks in plot is more than made up for in architectural riches. Alain Resnais creates a composite space by editing together scenes shot in a number of palaces and resorts around Munich: Schleissheim, Nymphenburg, Amalienburg, and so on. The film is plotless in two senses: it lacks both a clear narrative and a concrete geographical referent in the real world. Within the broad lineaments of film history, its slipperiness, its slackening of narrative cause-and-effect, is read as a symptom of its historical moment. The film occupies a special place in Gilles Deleuze's influential account of modern cinema's crisis of action, a crisis whose origins lay in the semiotic rubble of the Second World War.[6] But if we set our sights beyond the midcentury context of *Last Year at Marienbad* and stress continuity over change (repetition over difference?), we can come to appreciate the ways in which the cinematic hotel has continued to serve as a staging ground for ideas of transience, drift, and decentering, not least in the postmodern epoch explored in more recent independent cinema.

Last Year in Marienbad is an early example of a hotel film that articulates a kind of unplotting or unmooring, one that has little truck with the imperatives of narrative advancement. More recently, these films have sought to convey the affective intensities of drift on the one hand and an enthrallment to (or alienation from) the circuits of global capital on the other.[7] On this point, Caroline Levander and Matthew Guterl draw the reader's attention to the *metaspatial* function of hotels. Hotels are spaces that stage a point of entry into other spaces; they mediate their guest's relations to other (global) scales; and they "play a crucial role in architecting the larger geopolitical circuits that give shape, meaning, and texture to global capitalism and to the individual's relationship to it."[8] In what follows, I want to consider two American independent films, Sofia Coppola's *Lost in Translation* (2003) and Jim Jarmusch's *Mystery Train* (1989), that center on the space of the hotel to negotiate relationships between the local and the global, timelessness and anachronism. At stake in their cinematic meditations on being "lost in space," I argue, is a crucial tension between sameness and otherness.

* * *

Rem Koolhaas is not the only theorist to conceive of the experience of hotel dwelling in narrative terms, nor is he unique in turning to the hotel as a material expression of the historic shift from the modern to the postmodern. For instance, we might revisit Fredric Jameson's description of the Westin Bonaventure in Los Angeles as the apotheosis of postmodern architecture in *Postmodernism, or The Cultural Logic of Late Capitalism* (1991). Here he writes of the feeling of being lost in space, of a "milling confusion," when trying to find his coordinates in the mammoth hotel.[9] For Jameson this sense of disorientation rhymes with the disintegration of the subject in late capitalism. He credits the Bonaventure in particular with having "finally succeeded in transcending the capacities of the individual human body to locate itself, to organize its immediate surroundings perceptually, and cognitively to map its position in a mappable external world."[10] While Jameson's fascination is reserved for the vast proportions and architectural quirks of this particular landmark, hotels occupy an important place within postmodern thought more generally. Much of this stems from principles of metonymy; for Jameson, hotels function as "miniature cities," while for Peter Sloterdijk the hotel contains, in condensed form, the proposition for alternative forms of urban organization. Through their overarching forms of self-governance, hotels can appear bubble-like, self-contained, out of joint with the world that exists beyond their doors.

In thinking about the experience of being lost in space, another iconic Los Angeles hotel comes to mind: the Chateau Marmont, which features prominently in Sofia Coppola's *Somewhere* (2010). The Chateau Marmont is an imposing neo-Gothic hotel on Sunset Boulevard. It is somewhere that anybody who is somebody will have passed through at some point in their time in Los Angeles. The hotel's lush foliage and fortresslike enclosure offer its guests peace and quiet—a sanctuary from the restless gaze of the paparazzi. Coppola's film tells the story of one of its residents, Johnny Marco, who is in between shooting films and in a quiet period of his career in general. The bachelor-like existence enabled by his extended hotel stay is disrupted when his eleven-year-old daughter Cleo comes to stay with him. Her presence effects a subtle shift in emphasis and point of view that brings into relief the untenability of Johnny's hotel lifestyle and forces him to encounter a few home truths. *Somewhere* is also a film about the circulation of celebrity images and how such images become disconnected from reality.

Anna Backman Rodgers notes that "one of the most striking features of *Somewhere* is the manner in which the diegetic space is rendered as anonymous, sterile and transactional."[11] Coppola's vision of Los Angeles is "divested of its signification and is presented as a highly fragmented series of spaces that do not connect or cohere—indeed, in which it is hard to find one's coordinates."[12] Invoking the concept of the nonplace, a term coined by the anthropologist Marc Augé to describe those liminal spaces that entail a complex relation to time, space, and history within globalized supermodernity, she reads Coppola's crafting of cinematic space as an expression of a crisis in normative masculinity. In *Somewhere,* the Chateau Marmont and, more briefly, Milan's Principe de Savoia come to be defined negatively; these hotels are not houses, and they are definitely not homes. While their extended hotel residency is of a fundamentally different nature from the kind we find in *The Florida Project*, it is nonetheless correlated to an instability that Cleo finds increasingly unsettling, as, later, does Johnny. In one scene, Cleo cooks her father breakfast in an attempt to shore up a sense of domestic normality (an effort that is undermined by the fact that she relies on room service to source ingredients). And as the film reaches its end and Johnny "checks in" with himself emotionally, he makes the decision to check out of the Chateau Marmont definitively; the toxicity of a Hollywood lifestyle is deeply bound up with this space.

In Coppola's narrative universe—which is largely populated by white, wealthy, existentially unsettled drifters—hotels play a predictably important role. Her cinema is routinely described as "atmospheric," it explores social rituals, it attends to fallow time, and it tarries with the narratively inconsequential to bring affective subtleties to the surface. Her work, in other words, imparts a sense of how it might feel to dwell in spaces of hospitality that are the preserve of the privileged minority. Yet if the hotels that Coppola depicts cater frictionlessly to every whim, she also remind us that frictionlessness can lead to slippage, as her privileged protagonists frequently become untethered from real life. It is this sense of drift, figured as both potentiality and threat, that I want to explore as I turn to her earlier film, *Lost in Translation*. Here, too, she makes active use of the hotel to convey the rhythms and cadences of the postmodern subject's daily life.

* * *

Set in the Park Hyatt, a luxury hotel that sits atop the Shijuku Park Tower in central Tokyo, *Lost in Translation* explores the brief relationship between two of the hotel's guests: Bob, a B-list actor in his fifties, and Charlotte, a recent philosophy graduate in her early twenties. Bob's marriage is on the rocks, and his career is stalling (he is in Japan to advertise Suntory whiskey), while Charlotte has followed her emotionally vacant husband, a Los Angeles fashion photographer, to Tokyo on the off chance that she might find some direction in life. The two first exchange an incipient glance and a smile in the elevator and strike up a conversation in the hotel's piano bar. Through a series of brief encounters, Bob and Charlotte are drawn increasingly into one another's orbit. While the film lingers in a gray zone between friendship and attraction, Coppola ultimately thwarts "our generic expectation for sexual intimacy by playing with the hotel room spaces."[13] As with *I Can't Sleep*, a sense of vacancy permeates the film's atmosphere. The two central protagonists are drawn together by a string of shared afflictions: insomnia, jet lag, and racial, cultural, and existential unrest. The ground of their relationship, paradoxically, is a mutual sense of groundlessness.

The film's luxurious yet soulless hotel setting plays a key part in reinforcing its dominant affect. Prior to staging our entry into the Park Hyatt Tokyo, Coppola presents to us what Homay King memorably describes as "familiar signifiers for an unfamiliar Japan."[14] We follow Bob in a taxicab as he looks out to a glowing streetscape adorned by neon pictograms and walled in by digital screens. Unable to make sense of signs, he then encounters his own face atop a billboard. The effect is jarring, uncanny. While Bob hopes that the Park Hyatt will offer respite from the sensory exuberance of the twenty-four-hour city outside—an opportunity to decompress, away from a disorienting cityscape wrought by "space-time compression"—this will not be the case. While channel hopping, he is confronted anew by his own presence, this time dubbed in

Japanese; faxes arrive in the middle of the night; automated curtains rudely awaken him the morning after. This focus on automation, which is indexed to an undeniably racist vision of Japanese hypermodernity, increasingly places the taciturn Bob out of step with his surroundings and increasingly in step with Charlotte, who similarly grapples with her position as a foreign subject.

The hotel is a medium that stages a point of entry into a global imaginary. Discussing how hotels negotiate our relation to space and scale, Levander and Guterl note that they "let people know how much and what kinds of space they can take up in the world."[15] They take the example of the global hotel chain and explain how guests are afforded the right to "amble unfettered across vast expanses of heavily curated terrain, [thereby creating] a feeling, albeit temporary, of protection, vaccination, and domination."[16] Through their meticulously crafted aesthetics and architectural arrangement, such hotel chains negotiate our encounters with cultural alterity, offering either a thrilling proximity to, or a comforting distance from, the world that exists beyond the lobby.

In a series of shots that act as a visual refrain throughout the film, we watch Charlotte perching on the sill of her window, occupying a stance of repose. She sits, cocoonlike, with her knees close to her chest, casting a pensive glance up toward the sky or down onto the streets of Shinjuku below. When these shots occur in daylight, our attention is drawn to her body, which appears as if suspended at a vertiginous height above Tokyo. With the arrival of dusk, she becomes a silhouette. Our attention vacillates between the opaque contours of her body and the blue lights that hum in the cityscape below.

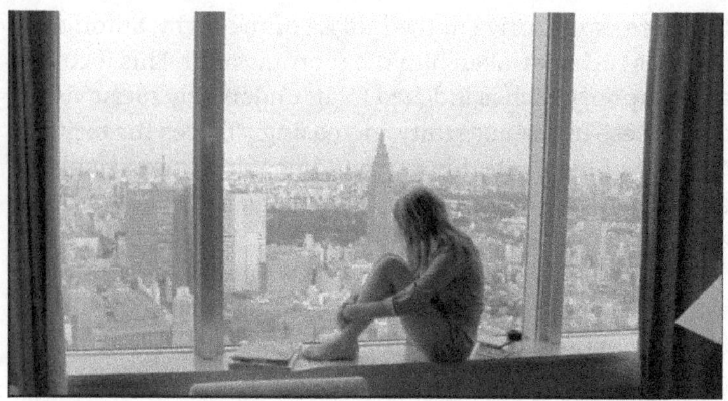

In these shots Coppola alternates between shallow and deep focus, centering and then decentering the human form. Through a purposeful mismatch of scales, the frames convey the contradictory sensation of being lost in space: Charlotte's bodily presence visually dwarfs the skyscrapers, but at the level of character psychology she feels insignificant. Neatly encapsulating a feeling that would come to emblematize Coppola's cinema in general, we get the impression here that the world exists at her fingertips, but the promise of plenitude feels strangely empty. For Robert Davidson, Coppola's cinematographic game of *fort/da* is a visual marker of the film's problematic engagement with space, place, and location: "For a split second, the city is briefly in focus, before the camera shifts to her, reducing Tokyo to a blurred, symptomatic vision of her ennui."[17] The geopolitical implications of Coppola's reductive treatment of Tokyo are explored further by Homay King, who situates Coppola's work within a much broader context of Western engagements with East Asia. *Lost*

in Translation, King argues, traffics in orientalizing clichés and 'Eastern' signifiers to broach questions of enigma, indecipherability, and opacity. More specifically, Charlotte conforms to the trope of the Western "lost girl" who looks to the East in search of philosophical consolation and spiritual counsel. In *Lost in Translation* her loss of direction is both metaphysical (she will lament to Bob, over drinks and cigarettes in the hotel bar, that her life lacks meaning) and all-too-literal (whole scenes will be dedicated to her wandering, aimlessly, through crowds in central Tokyo; we register the confusion on her face as she is unable to navigate Tokyo's subway system). In her account of the metaphor of spatial "orientation," Sara Ahmed shows how, at the level of the individual body, orientation refers to how people understand their sense of space, while on a macro level or a global register, the "Orient" conditions normative understandings of proximity and distance, sameness and difference.[18] By framing Tokyo as a site of spatio-temporal disorientation, Coppola's film is an object lesson in how spatial and psychic disorientation relies, implicitly, on the trope of the Orient to function.

The genesis of Coppola's film and the role that space plays in elaborating the narrative is revealing. Just as Japan was chosen because of the filmmaker's own familiarity with its defamiliarizing effects, so too the choice of the Park Hyatt derived from her own experience (as is also the case with the Chateau Marmont in her later work). As she explains: "Tokyo is so hectic, but inside the hotel it's very silent. And the design of it is interesting. It's weird to have this New York bar, the jazz singer, and the French restaurant, all in Tokyo. It's this weird combination of different cultures."[19] Bracketing for one moment the dubious cultural politics that seem to be at play here (would a Japanese restaurant in a Parisian hotel incur a similar charge of weirdness?), Coppola's statement invites us to consider why the space of the global hotel chain is such a propitious staging ground for a tale of postmodern alienation. As their names suggest, "global" or "intercontinental" hotel chains respond to a global clientele. At the level of aesthetics, then, their job is to aggregate tastes, catering to business and pleasure from the four corners of the world. While some hotels will introduce a small accent of a local culture in order to distinguish themselves from other nodes in the wider hospitality network, they necessarily tend, as Koolhaas argues, toward the generic.[20] In the case of *Lost in Translation*, it is this imperative to not alienate customers that Charlotte finds particularly alienating. The anaesthetizing dullness of the room reinforces her existential malaise. And while she will attempt to introduce a little color by affixing blossom-shaped paper ornaments to the light fixtures, these will have disappeared by the next day. A fire hazard, no doubt.

The tagline for Coppola's film reads: "Sometimes you have to go halfway around the world to come full circle." King understands the statement in narrative terms, writing that it "neatly encapsulates the way that the film sends Charlotte into a foreign territory, only to tuck her safely back under a familiar Oedipal wing"—a reference to Bob, who occupies an ambiguous position somewhere between love interest and father figure.[21] Yet I am tempted to take this invocation of travel a little more literally, moving us away from the provinces of Charlotte's mind and toward the territories of this film's geography. *Sometimes you have to go halfway around the world to come full circle.* Read differently, this line could be understood as a muted critique of the chain hotel as a generic space, one among many nodes in a global network that will constantly refer us back to the self-same, the already known. If, as the name suggests, *Lost in Translation* is a film that hinges on questions of sameness and difference—of feeling alienated by the sameness, or finding commonality in difference—then the Park Hyatt Tokyo is more than the neutral ground on which this tale is told. Given that *Lost in Translation* hews so closely to the bodies of two protagonists, cultural difference is largely externalized—it exists as a kind of abstract projection imputed to the "foreign" cityscape below or to Japanese bit parts who are far from fully fleshed characters. But what might a hotel film that is more hospitable to difference, porous, and open to cross-cultural intimacies look like?

* * *

Jim Jarmusch's 1989 *Mystery Train* shares several uncanny resonances with *Lost in Translation*. It is a film that also explores the cultural traffic between the United States and Japan, but Coppola's tourist trajectory is reversed. The first of the film's three acts follows two young backpackers, Mitsuko and Jun, who alight temporarily in Memphis as part of a tour of the South. As with *Lost in Translation*, the film functions as a cultural touchstone in thinking about symptoms of the postmodern condition (space-time compression, affective inertia, drift, ennui), and its focus on travel forces us to reckon with the unevenness of urban development at a global scale. As Thomas Carlson explains, "*Mystery Train* seems to offer us a strangely dehistoricized narrative peopled with characters who have little sense of temporal continuity or historical connection. They seem, that is, to suffer from what Jameson calls a 'schizophrenic' centeredness in a heightened present."[22] Both films follow people in states of crisis or transition.

Characters are beset by marital woes, oftentimes turning to bottles of whiskey for consolation. In both, the hotel serves as a space to temporarily house these concerns. Yet, while the clean surroundings and architectural rigor of the Park Hyatt Tokyo serve a kind of prophylactic function, curating certain exclusive forms of social experience while discouraging others, the Arcade Hotel that we encounter in *Mystery Train* is a $22-a-night flophouse that is amenable to strangers sharing a room and splitting the bill.

The relationship between Coppola's protagonists is framed as a question of character psychology. What does Charlotte see in Bob, and vice versa? Would we characterize their bond as amative, erotic, platonic, or forged by a shared sense of estrangement? What does he whisper to her as they bid each other goodbye? We can never be sure what it is that brings them together. Jarmusch, by contrast, is uninterested by such questions. His hotel, an altogether plainer establishment, is the locus of his film because it appears to be the only one open to the film's characters in downtown Memphis. It's a space of short-term dwelling for a diverse constituency of wayward figures. Yet the sense of humbleness and pragmatism that governs Jarmusch's film belies his sensitive attunement to what it means, and how it feels, to live as a postmodern subject. Like *Lost in Translation*, the film has excited and aggravated critics in equal measure for its lack of narrative resolution. But the empty moments, lack of coherence, and narrative divagations we find in *Mystery Train* are surely the point.

The film repeats a single day in Memphis from three perspectives. The first section, "Far from Yokohama," follows Mitsuko and Jun, who visit the city for a day. Enamored of rock and roll culture, they make a pilgrimage to the Sun

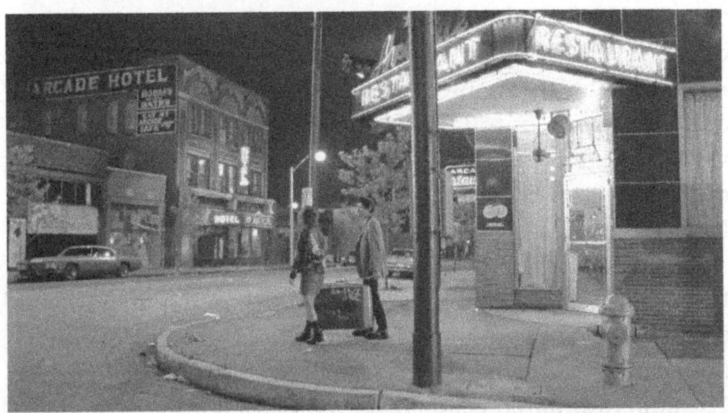

Records studio before spending their evening in the hotel. The second section, “A Ghost,” focuses on Luisa, an Italian woman who is stranded in Memphis while trying to repatriate her American husband’s remains. When she enters the Arcade Hotel she encounters DeeDee, who has just broken up with her boyfriend and needs a place to stay for the night. The two share a twin room, and Luisa encounters Elvis’s ghostly apparition in the dead of night. The third section, “Lost in Space,” follows DeeDee’s ex, an Englishman named Johnny, who drowns his sorrows in a dive bar with two friends. The inebriated men ramble through the streets of Memphis, ride around in a van, rob a liquor store, and crash for the night in the Arcade. In an altercation the morning after, Johnny accidentally shoots one of his friends, Charlie, in the leg, unleashing a gunshot whose sound will resonate like a common metronome across each of the stories.

Mystery Train is narratively threadbare. Like Coppola, Jarmusch is more interested in crafting moods and atmospheres than he is in coaxing disparate strands into something that coheres. While the film is routinely characterized as a "postmodern" film by virtue of its sketching of the uneven and anachronistic contours of America's cultural landscape, I would suggest that its loose multiplot form might also be described as an "incredulity toward metanarratives," to invoke Lyotard's phrasing.

Jarmusch has noted that the film's first section responded to his interest in how Japan's rapid urban expansion was outpacing that of the United States, thereby posing the question of how we might historicize the near past and the present. The superannuated vision of Memphis that Mitsuko and Jun had imagined prior to their arrival is replete with the signifiers of 1950s youth culture—Elvis Presley, Carl Perkins, rockabilly—yet these references have since calcified into historic clichés. The city in which they walk bears the ghost of another king—Martin Luther King—whose death on a balcony of the Lorraine Motel still casts a shadow over the town. We encounter downtown Memphis on foot, treading through potholes, weeds, and dwellings with nonspaces between them, empty and overgrown. Following a sequence of slow wide-angled panning shots, the couple stumble upon the Arcade Hotel, where vacancies are not in short supply. They take a room, painted in a duck-egg blue and adorned with a picture of Elvis. Mitsuko starts to take pictures of it; when Jun asks why she takes pictures of the unremarkable hotel interiors rather than the world outside, she responds, "Because the hotel and the airport are the things you do not remember." Much like Sophie Calle before her, she finds in the hotel room an observational gateway into the quotidian, and in the formal precision of photography a fitting means by which to register this proximate ethnography.

Whereas *Lost in Translation* relies on a crude binary opposition between cultures, Jarmusch offers a candid exploration of racial difference from multiple viewpoints. bell hooks draws particular attention the moment in the film in which the Japanese tourists exit the station and encounter "a homeless black man, a drifter . . . who turns to them and speaks in Japanese."[23] Of this brilliantly understated encounter, she writes: "This filmic moment challenges our perceptions of blackness by engaging in a process of defamiliarization (the taking of a familiar image and depicting it in such a way that we look at it and see it differently)."[24] Jarmusch goes on to explore the occluded racial politics that underpin many of the most successful U.S. cultural exports, chiefly via the motif of rock and roll music and the whitewashed vision of it that Jun and Mitsuko encounter.

The hotel comes to the fore of the film's exploration of race, labor relations, and Black life in the American South in the final section, where we follow a drunken conversation between the inebriated trio (the white Johnny and Charlie, and African American William Robinson) as they pass out in a free room in the Arcade. Commenting on the Elvis portraits that adorn every room, Johnny, himself an Elvis impersonator, questions why the singer's presence is so ubiquitous: "Why is he fuckin' everywhere? It's a Black hotel, in a Black neighborhood, with Black dudes working on the desk. Why don't they have a portrait of Otis Redding or Martin Luther King?" Will replies, "That's cause this is a *white-owned* hotel, they just got the brothers working." This questioning of appearances throws into relief how the racial logics of labor and property relations that we come to associate with the era of "The King" endure decades later. This is self-evident for Will but eludes the attention of his white friend. As the trio get increasingly drunk, throwaway comments mask moments of candor and profundity. As he gazes around the ramshackle room, his eyes glazing over, Will proclaims, "Lost in space, that's how I feel." The phrase refers both to the dizzying effects of liquor and also to the incommensurable gap between Will's own experiences and those of the two friends he dubs "snowflakes."

Lost in space. Will's choice phrase mounts an implicit challenge to how postmodern notions of "loss" and "drift" travels, frictionlessly, in the idiom of Coppola's universe. The idea of being "lost in space" resonates very differently for the Black male subject who wanders the streets of 1980s Memphis, who is subject to the routine indignities of police profiling and who feels a profound sense of deracination. While it may be tempting to align Will's sense of being "lost in space" with one of being "lost in translation," this would once again miss the racial blind spot in Coppola's film and to give in to the leveling of difference (the seductive farce of translation itself?).

While the two Western guests of Coppola's Park Hyatt Tokyo are drawn together through the mutual affliction of alienation in a film that translates this foreignness into a narratively legible commodity, the wayward subjects of Jarmusch's Arcade Hotel share little other than a common space and time. In spite of the postmodern "search for meaning" that is central to the two films, Jarmusch resists the temptation of false equivalence.[25] It is therefore telling that on the morning after the night in question Jun and Mitsuku (the protagonists of the film's first section) will *almost* bump into DeeDee (from the second) on their way to the station, but they narrowly avoid narrative overlap. While a hotel like the Arcade serves the purpose of "housing" the temporarily unhoused—sex workers, tourists, inebriated husbands, and wives who have been sent packing—neither these individuals nor we are asked to succumb to the consolations of an overarching narrative. The right to difference: Is this not another definition of hospitality?

4

Love Hotel

While Jim Jarmusch's Arcade Hotel houses three spatially contiguous narratives in a shared *timeframe*, some multiplot hotel films focus on the space of a single room as a point of continuity. A good example here is Eric Khoo's *In the Room* (2015), which presents a rich tapestry of stories unfolding in Room 27 of the fictional Singapura Hotel at various historical moments between the Second World War and a not-too-distant future. The opening black and white scene is a muted tale of queer intimacy between two men, one British and one Chinese, in the immediate aftermath of the fall of Singapore in 1942. In the second scene, in which the room has received a 1950s makeover (think amber, fuchsia, duck egg blue), we watch a brothel madame instruct four sex workers on the art of entertaining clients. Room 27 will then go on to host to a rock and roll sex party in the late 1960s; it will receive a Thai woman and her husband on the eve of her gender-affirming surgery in the '70s; it will serve as the setting for extramarital affairs in the '80s, and so forth. What ties together the scenes of Khoo's multiplot film, in other words, is not just a common setting but a shared theme. If the walls of Room 27 could talk, they would tell tales about sex. The ambitious aim of Khoo's drama is to condense over half a century of shifting approaches to gender and sexuality and contain it in the space of a single room.

Every day in every hotel, dirty linen is transformed into clean sheets. The traces of the previous night's bodies are removed. Through such processes of effacement, hotels sanction fleeting and anonymous intimacies. The injunction "Do Not Disturb" refers not only to the unwanted incursion of housekeeping staff into private rooms; it also signals a broader principle of hotel governance: discretion. In his essay "Sex and Hotels" Geoff Dyer makes a case for the hotel as a space of heightened eroticism. But for Dyer the sexiness of this space is not in fact predicated on any positive qualities. Rather, the hotel's sterility, impersonality, and starched white sheets gives its occupants carte blanche to engage in whatever they desire. "The sheets are clean, the toilets are clean, *everything* is clean, and this cleanliness is a flagrant inducement to—what else?—*filthiness*," he writes. The essay goes on to note how the blankness and impersonality creates a "cocoon" that is "sealed off from the outside world," where the minds of its occupants are focused squarely on bed-based activities. The temporary suspension of identity, as one relinquishes their passport, confers upon the hotel occupant "an ethical equivalent of diplomatic immunity" and a "moral weightlessness." While the political implications of Dyer's account of hotel sex trouble me insofar as they leave untroubled the implications of the "moral weightlessness" of the guest (frustratingly, his writing models the very same ethical equanimity that he confers on this essay's object), the tautological suggestion that hotel rooms "generate a special subset of room behavior that one might term hotel room behavior"—which he then goes on to name as "sex"—is a claim that I want to take up.[1] What role has cinema played in the circulation of fantasies about "hotel room behavior"?

Although a hotel room is not necessarily *only* a bedroom, its spatial relations are often oriented around a bed. For those hotels that court the trade of guests hoping to partake in bed-based activities beyond mere sleep, temporal relations come to be organized differently, too. Consider, for example, either the "Hotels of Assignation" that cropped up in the post–Civil War United States or the love hotels that have gained widespread popularity in Japan since the 1960s, where the question of how we parse the time of hotel occupation gains a surplus meaning. As Elizabeth Johnson notes of the love hotel, "rooms can be rented overnight (dubbed 'sleep/stay') or just for a few hours ('rest')."[2] In these establishments, which formalize the already deeply entwined relationship between hotel rooms and sex, "rest stops" and "rent-by-the-hour" models of room occupancy point to a sexual purpose that, somewhat paradoxically, feels both cloaked in euphemism and all too literal.

The affinities and tensions between cinema and the hotel become particularly striking when sex enters the equation. No doubt a reason for this is that cinema's logic of indexical capture is inimical to the working of a hotel, which, unlike the cinema, holds principles of discretion and impermanence in high regard. We might cast our minds back briefly to the case of Sophie Calle, who turned to photography to make public the otherwise private realm of the hotel room. Calle describes her surveillant gaze and artistic practice as a kind of "stealing by looking." (Indeed, while hotel management turn a blind eye to many illicit activities in the hotel, theft is not one of them.) And as we consider how the intimate lives and dirty laundry of strangers offers the artist irresistible narrative material, we might also cast our minds back to Rem Koolhaas's words that opened chapter 3: his suggestion that hotels "relieve the scriptwriter of the obligation of inventing a plot." A quick survey of the wealth of slapstick comedies set in hotels will tell you that the primary narrative trope to show up such "laziness" or "cheating" on the part of the scriptwriter is *cheating* itself.

Extramarital indiscretions are a dime a dozen in cinema's hotel narratives. Just think of Peter Glenville's 1966 comedy *Hotel Paradiso*, a film that uncannily foreshadows Koolhaas's claim. Here we encounter a playwright, Monsieur Feydeau (played by Glenville himself), who is searching for ideas for his next show and wrestling with writer's block. Feydeau checks into one of Paris's more disreputable "hotels of assignation." There he observes the serial philanderer, Boniface, who regularly meets up with his lover, Marcelle. It just so happens that her husband, Henri, who is blithely unaware of his wife's activities, is called to investigate rumors of ghosts in the hotel, only to find his wife in the arms of Boniface. After an ill-timed police raid, the hotel is revealed to be bursting at the seams with scenes of trysts, flings, and extramarital relations. While *Hotel Paradiso* is perhaps too farcical to make good on its trailer's promise of titillation (it is more of a comedy of errors than an erotic comedy), Glenville nonetheless lay bare the promiscuous traffic of semidressed bodies that move in and out of the hotel's rooms. What Koolhaas would later term the "collisions between human beings" is crudely, and carnally, literalized here.

* * *

One way to start thinking about the erotic life of the hotel is to approach the topic by way of a specific example. Between 1998 and 2000, star architect Jean Nouvel oversaw the design of Lucerne's "The Hotel." Though more modest in scale that some of his more notable works, it exhibits all the hallmarks of Nouvel's architectural signature. The Hotel's exterior is sympathetic to the surroundings of the lakeside town, retaining the plain but elegant nineteenth-century shell. But inside we find a striking interplay between building materials (a dark cherry wood and stainless steel), as well as the dramatic contrast between light and dark for which the architect is known.

A mere flip through glossy brochures, however, fails to give a full impression of Nouvel's project. Seen from a slightly different perspective—that of the hotel guest gazing up from their bed—another feature comes strikingly into view. As guests switch on the light directly above their bed, they are greeted by huge cinematic frescos, the twenty-five rooms replicating scenes from a dozen films. In a text that describes his vision for The Hotel, Nouvel explains that he wanted to recreate the "impression of escape in classical and Renaissance palaces," but to update this to the present day. "What are today's mythologies?" he asks, before answering that the "stories that everyone knows" now "come to us from the cinema, because cinema is our culture."[3]

Cinephilia is the governing principle of The Hotel. Guests staying in room 5700 are greeted by a shot from Stephen Frears's *Dangerous Liaisons* (1988) plastered on its ceiling. The design of the room produces an optical vacuum: the peach tone of Michelle Pfeiffer's skin is subtly referenced in the color of the walls, thereby drawing our eye upward. Similarly, in room 5100, the blue glow that clings to the torso of a strapping Brad Davis in Rainer Werner Fassbinder's *Querelle* is echoed in the color of the vintage accent chair. And the black, white, red, and jade that constitute the palette of room 5203 are lifted directly from Ōshima's *In the Realm of the Senses/Ai No Corrida*, which also commands our gaze as it occupies the totality of the ceiling space. Nouvel's favorite films dictate the bespoke design of every room. Each room's chosen film still unspools a new style, palate, and design.

Those familiar with Nouvel's architectural practice can attest that cinema is a recurrent motif in his oeuvre.[4] As a longtime collaborator explains: "Jean often uses film metaphors. That's because he creates sequences for his buildings. He wants the visitor to go through his buildings as though they were in a film, with different shooting sequences and emotions, accompanying every change of setting."[5] The itinerary that The Hotel offers through the history of art cinema and the Freudian recesses of its creator's head is decidedly sexual, given that each of these frescos refers its guest-spectators back to what Dyer calls "hotel room behavior." Even the hotel's restaurant, bar, and its external facade exude eroticism. As architectural theorist Donald Albrecht writes: "Nouvel mixes mirrors, movie stills, and windows to alternately hide and reveal public spaces, like a sexy striptease."[6]

There is a curious disconnect between the overt eroticism of Nouvel's references and the hotel management's sanitized presentation of this space via promotional materials and online platforms. For instance, the website boasts of creating the hotel equivalent of "taking a dream journey through the *big-screen epics* of cinematic history." Such language leads us toward a misleadingly mainstream and chaste impression of the cinematic history on display. (*In the Realm of the Senses* was famously banned from the big screen in Ōshima's native Japan, as well as many other countries, at the time of its release.) The official discourse surrounding The Hotel offers a negative index of the friction between Nouvel's daring cinematic imaginary and the business imperatives of the chain that now manages it. As I noted in the previous chapter, cosmopolitan hotel chains are, after all, in the business of aggregating tastes, neutralizing tensions, and appealing to diverse markets. Put simply, it makes good business sense to usher sexually explicit content into the realm of connotation.

Seen through the eyes of the cinephile for whom Nouvel's references were presumably originally intended, then, one cannot help but wonder whether The Hotel serves the role of a Trojan horse. For while, on first glance, it is the formal signatures and credentials of the architect that ostensibly distinguish Nouvel's building from the prestige hotels that act as its direct competition, on closer inspection the hotel's distinction lies in the perverse (albeit often cryptic) cinematic references that are smuggled into its rooms.

Some rooms (and films) come with a lot of baggage. Consider Bernardo Bertolucci's risqué erotic drama *Last Tango in Paris* (1972), which tells of the sexual exploits of a hotel owner, played by Marlon Brando, who pursues anonymous sexual relations with a young Parisian woman, played by Maria Schneider. The film—which forms the basis for Room 5402's decor—famously skirted the edge between art cinema and erotica in the early 1970s, only to be outdone a few years later by a film whose images Nouvel plasters on the ceiling of three other rooms.

So let us now dwell for a moment with *In the Realm of the Senses*, whose "sensuous ceiling picture encourages far-reaching thoughts," according to the copy on The Hotel's website. Ōshima's controversial erotic art film tells the tale of Sade Abe, a former sex worker, now a chambermaid, who works in a traditional Ryokan hotel in 1930s Tokyo. There she encounters the owner Kichizō Ishida, who oversees the geishas working in the establishment, and initiates a string of sexual activities with her that will soon take on a momentum of their own as they flee to the countryside and take up lodgings in similar establishments.

Since the film's release, *In the Realm of the Senses* has generated much anxious discussion about where it sits on the spectrum from art cinema to pornography. (Much of this commentary has been limited, unimaginatively, to Ōshima's use of unsimulated sex scenes.) But what strikes me as more interesting is how the film's provocative blurring of generic boundaries come to be played out spatially. In an early sex scene, which takes place on the wraparound porch, we watch Sada sit atop Kichizō. Following a close-up on her poppy red kimono, which is ruffled by her lover's fumbling hands, the camera cuts to a long shot that also contains an elderly woman dusting a statue on the other side of the courtyard. At another memorable midcoital moment, we watch Kichizō breaking a glass window to create a hole through which he will communicate with a geisha who waits patiently outside. What arrests our attention here is not necessarily the sex act, but rather the temporary shattering of the film's pornotopic logic to show other, more banal, activities also taking place.[7] By approaching this film through the prism of space we come to a greater appreciation of how the architectural features of the

Ryokan (such as its thin walls, sliding doors, and semipublic courtyard areas) are key to constructing and navigating the film's thresholds of sensual intensity.

If the film advances an understanding of temporary dwelling spaces as spheres that exist outside of the purview of conjugal relations (spaces marked by "moral weightlessness" as Dyer puts it), then this is not to suggest that the activities that occur within them are without consequence. Pleading to his lover, Kichizo says, "I'll promise to set you up in an inn," to which Sada responds, "I don't want to be your mistress, I want you all the time." The full extent of her wish for possession will not become clear until the film's ending. The vicissitudes of their sexual exploits reach new levels of intensity, and their graphic exploration of each other's bodies culminates with a string of crimes of passion: dismemberment, strangulation, and ultimately murder. Although we are spared the gruesome details of these actions in the frescos that adorn the ceilings of Nouvel's Hotel, this might strike us as an odd sign under which to place the occupants of the King Deluxe Studio.

The cinephile who continues to wander through the floorplan of The Hotel will quickly learn that the corpus on which Nouvel draws is very much an *anti*-honeymoon suite of films. From Patricia Rozema's *When Night Is Falling* and Bertolucci's *The Sheltering Sky* through to Stephen Frears's *Dangerous Liaisons*, a common denominator among The Hotel's references is a failing marriage. By projecting these eroticized images onto the ceilings of The Hotel's rooms, Nouvel is making an implicit claim (a projection?) about guests' own erotic object choices. Given that the rooms are typically quite dark, guests are invited to engage with their rooms in a way that mimics the working of the cinematic apparatus itself. With the flick of a bedside switch, the ceiling frescos are illuminated. The images make a claim on our attention, and perhaps invite us to attend to carnal pleasures of our own. Yet for the restless guest-spectator who lingers with these images once the initial frisson of excitement has subsided, or for the cinephile who traces these glossy images back to their diegetic source, the results may be unsettling. The implicit risk in Nouvel's suggestive coupling of cinema and the hotel is that this might, over time, transpire to have been a dangerous liaison.

* * *

Pornography is often filmed in hotels, as both setting and set. Since the late 1980s, Los Angeles photographer Jeff Burton has worked in the San Fernando Valley to document pornography's mode of production. His *Dreamland* series attends to the settings of porn shoots, from the rented houses of the Los Angeles nouveaux riches through to louche hotel suites, bringing into focus the lifeworld that typically recedes from view in pornography's production. Writing in a decidedly elegiac tone, Neville Wakefield notes how the series "documents this edge where pornography locates the real fictions of Pop amongst the debris of a mainstream long since curdled into special effect."[8]

In their accounts of how adult media offers us a rich historical archive of material culture, feminist scholars Jennifer Wicke and Elena Gorfinkel, respectively, have both paid close attention to the roles that interior design, decoration, furnishings, and accessories play in erotic cinema. "Bedroom props," Wicke writes, "only have to be a shade off to sunder any sexual response to the pictures, and instead open up a reverie on the punctum of any particular image."[9] For Gorfinkel a room's decor is not ancillary to the sensory pleasures of vintage pornography; rather, these details are consubstantial with adult media's very allure insofar as they exhibit the traces of a past world, a superannuated fantasy of "dated sexuality."[10]

Burton's photographs turn away from the "action" of pornography to attend to those small details—objects, furnishings—that crystallize the historicity of pornography's image repertoire, attuning us to a fast-receding past. A sex scene involving two upright men and a woman laid on a table, redolent of the scenes of appetitive excess and bacchanalian debauchery we find in Marco Ferreri's *The Big Feast* (*La grande bouffe*, 1973), will find itself trumped by the silver meat dome to the left of the copulating bodies. Another image, more tightly focused on a hotel room, further splinters our spectatorial attention: in the top right hangs a kitsch painting of a man on a horse, descending from the heavens; to the left is an ornamental lamp; and in the bottom left a mirrored surface on the bed's headboard captures the ass of a man who penetrates a second body that remains just out of view. As we look at this photograph, the intended object of our gaze is unstable: as we toggle between the photograph's competing focal points, we move between a series of perceptual states, ranging from ribald laughter (at the visual resonances between sex and horseback riding) through to more measured, formally attentive form of reception typically reserved for a very different category of ready-made objects. Not only do the ephemeral details of private rooms and hotel suites often serve as a fleeting source of visual fascination, but Burton's oblique framing of these erotic spaces works to destabilize the ontological order of things that the well-oiled machine of pornographic production so laboriously seeks to affirm. Somewhat in tension with Dyer's earlier argument that it is the hotel room's qualities of emptiness and anonymity that accentuate its sexiness, Burton reveals how these interior backdrops might body forth from the recesses of insignificance to play a crucial role in the hotel's erotic promise.

The logic of displacement that Burton's photographs enact find a counterpart in a film by Mexican American filmmaker Naomi Uman, though this time the pornographic source is of a different vintage. In her short film *removed* (1999), Uman turned her attention to the archives of 1970s pornography to work through similar questions about how and where we look when we consume adult media. Uman's *removed* reworks celluloid fragments from *Swingin' Models* (1972), a West German softcore film. In one of the scenes in the original film, a weary young couple attend a swinging party in a luxurious "bordello" hosted by the wealthy pornographer and his wife. Later into the evening, the couple abandon their plan to travel home on the icy roads and accept the offer of a room for the night. Unbeknownst to them, the suite contains a two-way mirror which will allow the hosts to spy on the couple (thereby enacting the same sordid scheme that would gain widespread notoriety in the motel-based documentary *Voyeur*, based on the writing of Gay Talese). In the scene that Uman selects for her film, we listen to the host describe the scene of nudity that is unfolding in front of his eyes to his wife, who writhes on her own bed and moans in pleasure.

In her tactile reworking of the found footage, Uman used a combination of nail polish and bleach to remove the female bodies from each side of the mirror. *removed* brings into view a rough, scratchy, unstable burst of light where female forms once existed, accompanied by the ekphrastic descriptions of the eroticized bodies that we find in the source text. While it is perhaps tempting to read Uman's film through the prism of, or as an artistic response to, Laura Mulvey's account of the "to-be-looked-at-ness" of women's bodies in her essay "Visual Pleasure and the Narrative Cinema," I join others in thinking that *removed* isn't necessarily cut to the measure of Mulvey's theoretical model.[11] For me, the curious oscillation between figure and ground that is occasioned by this perceptual object also brings into relief the 1970s mise-en-scène—gaudy lampshades, vintage wall décor—that is consubstantial with (rather than a stubborn impediment to) the aesthetic pleasures of these images. The instability of Uman's images, in other words, invites us to think about the relationship between copulating bodies and the trappings of style and décor in less strictly oppositional terms.

* * *

Hotels are not only spaces of pornographic production; they are also important sites of its consumption.[12] The story of pornographic film's entry into, and circulation within, hotel rooms worldwide is a curious one, whose origins reveal much about the cosmopolitanism of the hotel form and the contingency of adult media's dissemination.

In 1970s Japan, rent-by-the-hour love hotels were booming in popularity in response to the particularities of domestic life in urban centers. The paper-thin walls of apartments and the multigenerational makeup of many households made it difficult for occupants to discretely have sex. Love hotels effectively rezoned the bedroom into the space of a hotel. As part of their offering, these establishments often screened adult films in their rooms by way of closed-circuit video systems. However, one day in 1971, this technology went awry. An Osaka hotel's video system accidentally converted a steel railing on the rooftop into an antenna that transmitted the "pink movie" to televisions in neighboring houses, which prompted a stern police warning.[13] The unfortunate incident received a writeup in a March 1971 edition of *Time* magazine with the title "Sinerama in Osaka."[14] As the story made its way across the Pacific, it would have an important ripple effect. As adult film historian Peter Alilunas explains, one of the readers of the article was Don Leon, a Californian lawyer representing motel owners who saw a gap in the U.S. hospitality market. While pay-per-view models of film viewing in hotels were growing increasingly popular in the early 1970s, pornography was not yet an offering, not least because of a fear among innkeepers that its presence would be perceived as lending tacit approval to sex work. Alilunas goes on to describe how Leon convinced the group of motel owners that he represented to "convert an AutoLodge at 930 West Olympic Boulevard, downtown near the convention center, into an 'adult motel,' complete with water beds, fur bedspreads, mirrored ceilings, and closed-circuit adult films played on Sony U-Matic machines," thereby paving the way for the on-demand model of adult media consumption we know to this day.[15]

* * *

As I trace the role that the love hotel plays in adult media's circulation and proliferation, I am reminded of a sequence from Gaspar Noé's 2009 film, *Enter the Void*, in which we, the film's disembodied spectators, temporarily alight on a Tokyo love hotel. The first part of the film fuses our own vision to the perceptual apparatus of Oscar, a low level drug dealer and twenty-something American living in Tokyo. Following his sudden death in a drug bust, the first-person gaze undergoes a transmutation—we leave his fleshy mortal body behind and follow his immaterial spirit on a vertiginous trip as his consciousness roams freely through the streets of Tokyo in search of his sister, Linda.

As its title suggests (and the Freudian fever dream that constitutes Noé's back catalogue further attests), *Enter the Void* frequently gravitates toward holes. As part of the film's disorienting plunge into the Tokyo underworld, we reach a love hotel. The building's facade pulses with holographic tiles, piquing the magpie sensibility we have come to cultivate over the course of the film. A neon sign beckons us in. We enter through a fourth story window and watch from above a couple caught midcoitus before the camera wanders into another room where sex is also taking place. The corridor that connects the rooms is lined with a red light, fittingly reminiscent of an airport landing strip. Our gaze follows Oscar's lines of flight, his trajectory of desire, as it passes through walls to reveal people engaged in sexual acts. Like a moth, he is drawn to the glow of libidinal energy that radiates

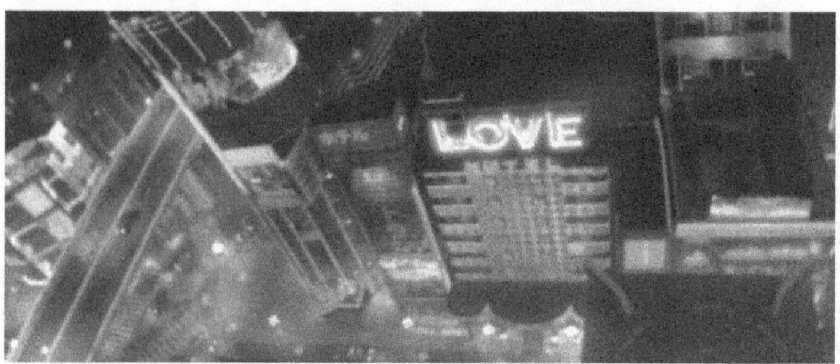

from bodies. Hotels—and love hotels in particular—are supposed to adhere to a logic of discretion, carefully partitioning public and private zones. Noé upsets this spatial logic.

In this scene, which surveys a vast topography of copulating bodies, Noé combined on-location shooting with scenes that were produced in a studio with the use of cranes before later augmenting this footage in an intensive postproduction process that lasted over a year. Yet in spite of the scene's technical ingenuity and visual pyrotechnics, my own patience toward this spectacle soon wears thin. While Noé, one of European art cinema's *enfants terribles*, is obviously courting notoriety with such a cinema of carnal attractions, to emphasize the film's transgressivness risks forgetting what the long history of cinema's engagement with the hotel can tell us: that there is nothing particularly novel about a director's wish to play "Peeping Tom" and transgress the supposedly private space of the hotel. Although the sex scenes in the love hotel exhibit significant technical prowess—floating gracefully between rooms in a dazzling display of cinematic movement and visual effects—such novelty belies the fact that Noé is rehashing a trope from the days of early cinema: the voyeuristic motif of the "through-the-keyhole" drama.

The through-the-keyhole drama was an important and historically significant type of film that can be traced back to the early 1900s, when filmmakers sought to show what was typically hidden behind the doors of hotel rooms.[16] The pleasures and anxieties of spectatorship in these early films was predicated on the access that its viewers were granted to spaces and scenarios that had hitherto been private. In Ferdinand Zecca's *Par la trou de serrure/Through the Keyhole* (1902), for example, we follow a hotel porter and voyeur who looks through the keyholes of four different rooms, only to be noticed by the occupant of the final room, who subsequently kicks him down the stairs. These crudely diagrammed sexual dynamics are later reversed in Ladislaw Starewicz's *The Cameraman's Revenge* (*Mest' kinematograficheskogo operatora*, 1912), a stop-motion film in which the characters are played by dried insect speciments. Here a restless Mr. Beetle leaves his doting wife at home to spend some time in the city, where he pursues a dragonfly working as a cabaret dancer. In the bar he has an altercation with a grasshopper—the eponymous cameraman—who later follows the beetle and the dragonfly to the "Hotel d'Amour," capturing the beetle's indiscretions through their hotel keyhole. Here our peeping Tom exacts his revenge; the compromising footage is later screened in a cinema that Mr. and Mrs. Beetle later frequent, thereby leading to public scandal and marital acrimony.

These keyhole dramas intuitively grasp the dialectical nature of spatial, sexual, and spectatorial relations—the logic of the burlesque. The relation between seer and seen is cunningly calibrated to full dramatic effect, eliciting the attention and stoking the curiosity of the prurient viewer, only to somehow frustrate the *passage à l'acte*. In Zecca's case, the peeping Tom is caught and expelled. By contrast, Noé's omniscient gaze, which glides frictionlessly across the hotel's thresholds, achieves a very different effect. Once the "penetration of rooms" starts to lose its dramatic effect, *Enter the Void* resorts to penetration tout court.[17] We are gradually drawn into the orbit of a copulating couple, Linda (Oscar's sister) and Alex (his best friend). In a further shift of scale, our gaze assumes an endoscopic function, as we follow the fluids that pass from Alex and into Linda, returning us to "The Origin of the World" (a nod to Courbet, a metonym for the French avant-garde tradition out of which Noé, too, would later be born).[18]

The lesson that *Enter the Void* imparts to us about hotel sex is one that we grasp by way of negative instruction: that the mere *potentiality* of sex taking place in the space of the hotel is often more interesting than the act itself. *Enter the Void* is beholden to a positivist epistemology; it is obsessed with the money shot. By contrast, "through-the-keyhole" dramas, which play peekaboo with erotic bodies, make more active use of the hotel's own architectural forms—the tension between enclosure and disclosure, the play between visibility and invisibility—in ways that bring the hotel itself to the fore of desiring relations.

While the most remarked upon aspect of *Enter the Void*'s hotel scene—its endoscopic exploration of bodily interiors—might call to mind the more infamous and visceral work of American experimental filmmaker Stan Brakhage,[19] there is another more subterranean connection between the two filmmakers that brings the question of hotel eroticism more squarely into view. In the early 1970s Brakhage embarked on a series of films that he named the "Sexual Meditation" cycle. These films, most of which were shot in 16mm, range between three and six minutes in length and explore the erotic charge of everyday spaces. In Brakhage's own words, *Sexual Meditation: Hotel* (1972) "takes its cues from that ultimate situation of SEX MED./masturbation—the loft-and-lonely hotel room." Tellingly, the space of the hotel benefits from a longer and more complex treatment than the settings of the other films in the cycle: an office suite, a motel, a field, a room at Yale University.

Sexual Meditation: Hotel succeeds in piquing my curiosity, whereas *Enter the Void* largely fails. For, while Noé's "show all" approach to hotel interiors leaves little to the imagination, the visual grammar of Brakhage's *Hotel* is subtle and tantalizing. The experimental short is ostensibly set in a hotel room that overlooks a similar establishment, though the ill-defined images and liberal use of close-ups thwart any possibility of visual or spatial mastery. *Hotel* presents a patchwork of images, ranging from shots of TV static and test patterns, close-ups of body parts, architectural details, and shots looking outside of a window and into the hotel opposite. Brakhage's homage to the "loft-and-lonely hotel room" throbs and pulses with an erotic energy. Haptic close-ups transform the surfaces of walls into something resembling flesh; framed from a particular angle, the textiles in the room across the way resemble close-ups of a body; the curved edge of the top of an antique fabric lampshade resembles the contour of a bustier. Brakhage's camera not only animates previously inanimate things but also eroticizes them in a coy but suggestive game of peekaboo. The forms that we encounter are always on the verge of coalescing into legible images, only for the camera to cut to another form. By framing objects from oblique angles, the film transforms the hotel room's manifold surfaces, details, and objects into a sort of erotic Rorschach test. Brakhage returns to the spectatorial relation and the hotel encounter a dialectical tension—a play of subject and object, public and private—that is dispensed with entirely in *Enter the Void*. Unlike the crisp images, and the smooth movements across hotel space that we find in Noé's film, Brakhage's grainy images, erratic editing, and frustrated movement through space engenders a sensation of friction, and a frisson of the illicit. Yet while Brakhage suffuses the hotel with an erotic charge, and succumbs to what Dyer calls the "flagrant inducement to *filthiness*" in the hotel, the preponderance of fetishized close-ups of women's bodies in his Sexual Meditation cycle reveal the familiar contours of the filmmaker's male heterosexual visual economy.[20] What, we might wonder, could a queer feminist erotics of the hotel look like?

* * *

The hotel is a staple of Chantal Akerman's cinema. It acts as a waystation for the many exilic subjects that wander in and out of her cinematic universe. Akerman's first treatment of the hotel was undertaken around the same time as that of Brakhage. In 1972 she made *Hotel Monterey*, a slow meditation on the life of a run-down hotel in Manhattan. Filmed over the course of a single day, Babette Mangolte's camera roams the space of the residential hotel from the ground floor lobby to empty corridors and upward to a rooftop, advancing at a glacial pace not out of step with those of the elderly residents we see shuffling in and out of the frame at various points. Though there was nothing particularly queer about *Hotel Monterey* (except, perhaps, its mode of conception, having been financed from money that Akerman had pocketed when working in New York's 55th Street Playhouse, a gay porn theater), her patient study of the transience of hotel life, the footfall of anonymous strangers, and themes of intimacy, contact, and desire would go on to pave the way for a more avowedly queer imagining of hotel space a few years later.

Les rendez-vous d'Anna/The Meetings of Anna (1978) follows Anna, a Belgian filmmaker and a thinly veiled stand-in for Akerman herself, who travels from Essen in West Germany to Brussels and through to Paris to attend a program of screenings and press events over the course of a few days and nights. Anna stays in a succession of hotel rooms. Like her previous film, *The Meetings of Anna* is also a hymn to the lulling cadences of hotel life. The camera often lingers on the suite's plain furnishings, or frames Anna looking vacantly out a window, as if momentarily transported into the realm of an Edward Hopper painting, before she welcomes in men to occupy her bed for the night. The sex that transpires in these rooms is often detached, affectless, and most often unfinished. Though sexual climax is rarely reached in the film, it has been widely praised for its representation of casual sex, perhaps by virtue of its lack of sentimentalism and its failure to conform to heavily gendered scripts of erotic and emotional attachment. Akerman doesn't yield to the demands of her more impatient spectators; her film's refusal to succumb to the insistence for psychological transparency and to traffic in the habitual signifiers of cinematic desire can be understood as part of a feminist ethics of opacity.[21]

Midway through the film, Anna arrives in the Gare du Midi in her hometown of Brussels and meets her mother for a coffee. The two decide to spend an evening in the hotel, sharing a bed, before the filmmaker continues to Paris in the morning. In the dead of night, she tells her mother about a brief tryst she had with an Italian woman. It started with a stray hand, then a momentary touch, then a hesitant kiss, and then Anna and her lover found themselves swept up in an all-consuming passion. She confesses that she thought of her mother during her sexual awakening, to which her mother responds, plainly, that she will not tell Anna's father. The naked Anna nestles up against her as the scene draws to a close. The first time I watched this scene I was struck by its sensuality, its gradual erosion of the distinction between maternal affection and eroticism. It turns out that I was far from alone in this impression: Marion Schmid sees in this the scene a "tight intertwin[ing]" of lesbian love and maternal bonding that acts as a tender counterpoint to the (hetero) sexual disappointment depicted elsewhere in the film; B. Ruby Rich, who compares this encounter with the film's more explicit scenes of hetero copulation, also proclaims this the film's "hottest moment."[22]

The temporary melding of identities between the mother, played by Lea Massari, and this Italian lover is not just a figment of Anna's erotic imagination. Rather, it is further illuminated when we situate Akerman's film within a broader constellation of European art cinema. Massari first came to prominence in 1960 for her role as a young Italian woman, also named Anna, who goes missing in Michelangelo Antonioni's *L'Avventura*. Akerman ends *The Meetings of Anna* with her protagonist, played by Aurore Clément, listening to a voicemail asking, "*Anna, Dove sei?*" (Anna, where are you?), representing a quite literal callback to an earlier moment in cinema's history. But the film's intertextual knots do not end there. Lea Massari had previously gained notoriety for her role in Louis Malle's *Murmur of the Heart* (*Le souffle au coeur*, 1971). Here she played Clara, the troubled and adulterous mother of a sexually precocious and unruly fourteen-year-old boy named Laurent. Following the development of her son's heart condition, which necessitates a trip to a sanatorium, Clara and Laurent are mistakenly booked into a single hotel room for the duration of their stay. Dwelling in close quarters and unable to maintain their habitual privacy, the hotel room becomes a crucible of psychosexual experimentation. By the film's end they will end up having sex, thereby consummating the Oedipal transgression to which Akerman will gesture—only mutely—in her own film. So as we return to the Brussels hotel room that forms the erotic locus of *The Meetings of Anna*, it is not so simple to frame this setting as one that exists outside of habitual domestic routines and the strictures of the patriarchal law. Rather, by way of the intertextually resonant screen presence of Massari, the hotel room becomes queerly inflected. It is a space of tenderness and maternal bonding. But it is also a realm of polymorphous desire.

5

Chelsea Ghosts

The hotel is a rich example of what cultural historian Pierre Nora terms a *realm of memory*: a living archive, a physical site that contains the accretions of history, a space in which layers of memories coalesce and intersect. However, the maintenance of these spaces often runs counter to these processes; for what is hotel upkeep if not a kind of letting go of past presences, a cleaning up or wiping away of the stubborn marks of previous occupation?

Some of the earliest sightings of the hotel in cinema dramatize this tension to fantastical effect by turning to the spectral figure of the ghost. J. Stuart Blackton's *The Haunted Hotel* (1907), for example, one of the oldest surviving films, tells the tale of a weary traveler who arrives at an inn in the countryside. Once he checks in a housekeeper brings him an evening meal. But at the dinner table things start to go awry: a knife hovers above a loaf of bread before cutting it, a coffee pot pours itself, a sprite springs from the spout of a milk jug. The bewildered guest goes to sleep, only to be visited by ghouls who dance in a ring around his bed. The film takes a fantastical turn, and a demon grabs the traveler from his bed. Stuart

Blackton created the special effect of ghostly presence by using a process of double exposure, wherein the aperture of the camera allows light to pass through the lens and onto the photochemical substrate more than once, a technique commonly used by spirit photographers. Given that *The Haunted Hotel* is also an early experiment in stop-motion animation, many of the improbable movements depicted on screen are the product of invisible hands laboring offscreen.

The smooth operation of the hotel is also at stake in Segundo de Chómon's film *El Hotel Eléctrico* from the following year. Here we watch two patrons, a man and a woman, dwelling in an upmarket hotel whose services are fully automated and powered by electricity; a levitating brush shines shoes and styles hair, a free-floating pen will write letters on their behalf. Although the film's activities are framed as technical feats rather than supernatural tricks, here again we encounter ghosts in the hotel by way of a ghost in the machine. The electric hotel takes on a life of its own: whirling lines, painted by hand, are superimposed onto frames of the hotel's central machine as if to suggest a state of disarray, and both furniture and guests will be dragged into a dizzying vortex before the film abruptly cuts to the end.

Both examples tell us something about cinema's enduring fascination with ghosts. While much early discourse on cinema hailed it as a technical novelty, the apex of rational modernity, the medium also carried with it a mystical, oneiric, ineluctable surplus. James Cahill writes that "ghosts encompass cinema's forms of absent presence, temporal disjunctions and anachronisms, and uncanny effects produced by and fostered in cinema."[1] Since its earliest days, cinema in turn has propagated the idea that hotels are haunted by ghosts, whether in the form of the absent presence of prior guests, whose traces may be effaced save only the fading ink on the pages of a guestbook, or a contingent body of cleaning staff, whose names might not appear on any paperwork whatsoever.

A brief internet search of "haunted hotels" yields a familiar set of results that in and of itself attests to the role that cinema plays in sustaining the hotel imaginary. Recurring examples include the Cecil Hotel (a run-down and now-defunct Los Angeles hotel, the subject of a hit Netflix documentary); the Stanley Hotel, Colorado (the setting of Kubrick's *The Shining*); and New York's Chelsea Hotel (which, while itself the subject and setting of a low-budget horror film, resonates with a greater force outside of these generic parameters). Once a space of bold utopian reimagining, and now a site of melancholy retrospection, it is perhaps fitting that the Chelsea Hotel and the cinematic ghosts that inhabit it should serve as this book's final destination.

* * *

Built in the late 1880s by architect Philip Hubert, a disciple of utopian theorist Charles Fourier, the Chelsea Hotel has a spirit of social experimentation and an ethos of collective living etched into its DNA.[2] Early on in the twentieth century it served as a meeting point for artists and travelers who would live in close quarters. From the 1960s onward, during the tenure of renowned hotelier Stanley Bard, it gained a reputation as a bohemian petri dish, generating its own distinct counterculture.

Though a refuge for artists working in—or, perhaps more important, across—a variety of art forms, the specifically cinematic genealogy of the Chelsea is a rich one which takes us on a dizzying journey through time and space, from early

U.S. documentary and avant-garde cinema to the French *cinéma du look* (*Léon*, Luc Besson, 1994) and Japanese horror on a shoestring (*Hotel Chelsea*, Jorge Valdés-Iga and Hiro Masuda, 2009). Moreover, the hotel counts among its former residents such figures as pioneering documentarian Robert Flaherty; experimental filmmaker Jonas Mekas, whose 1967 short film *I Leave the Chelsea* shows him departing from the hotel with a copy of *Film Culture* in hand before revealing a historic plaque bearing Flaherty's name; and, of course, Andy Warhol, whose *Chelsea Girls* (1966) adopts a double-projection format to convey a sense of the simultaneity of social interactions among the film's superstar cast. But while the Chelsea is a tempting spot for indulging in cinetouristic sightseeing, a whistle-stop tour is not one that I am particularly interested in rehearsing here, not least because this would run counter to the hotel's putative ethos of holding open a space for those who inhabit the margins. For while the names of certain figures associated with the Chelsea become sedimented through bohemian mythologization, other figures in this cinematic avant-garde, such as Harry Smith and Shirley Clarke, deserve a wider audience.

A regular in the hotel since the 1960s, artist and polymath Harry Smith contributed to the propagation of occult and mysticist thinking in the Chelsea. Like the early cinema examples with which this chapter opened, his *Film No. 12* (later renamed *Heaven and Earth Magic* by Jonas Mekas) is an oneiric film, abounding with skeletons and ghostly apparitions, and a work of stop-motion animation. Most of the moving objects we encounter in this animation seem to float freely, unanchored from any definite spatial parameters. The unfolding of the surreal film recalls the principle of the exquisite corpse:

bodies are constantly transmuting into other forms, objects interact in a bewildering play of scale, size, and signification. Given that the film resists straightforward exegesis, critics tend to seize upon a moment, roughly a sixth of the way into the film, in which the film's mind resembles the space of a room. Behind the silhouette of a woman's head emerges the outline of a room's walls and ceiling; the contours of Euclidean space in a sense *domesticate*, or momentarily contain, the objects that dance across the screen. In the middle of the screen stands the torso of a mannequin—a homunculus, of sorts—whose erratic gestures summon floating objects. The sequence unfolds against a buzzing soundscape of bells, alarms, rattling sounds, the occasional howl of a dog. While critic John L. Waters describes Smith's musique concrète score as the "sort of soundtrack you could put together in a hotel room," I would suggest that if any trace of the Chelsea is inscribed in this film then this is likely to be apprehended visually. *Heaven and Earth Magic* presents a bricolage aesthetic. The film combines elements of modernist graphic design, a steampunk predilection for industrial machinery, and a nod to Victorian aesthetics by way of the paper cutouts that Smith sourced from nineteenth-century catalogues. (This is to say, it mutely registers a debt to the place in which the film was, in part, pieced together.) As the many guests to his Chelsea "salon" attest, Smith was a voracious collector and amateur anthropologist—his room, like this film, was filled to the brim with stuff. Nesting between the weighty piles of books and records that he kept in his lodgings were collections of paper planes gleaned from gutters of the Bowery, crushed Coke cans, Ukrainian easter eggs, and Seminole textiles (the latter collection would feed directly into his *Film No. 15*.)

In the 1970s, with his turn away from abstraction, Smith produced a film that shone a light on the Chelsea's vibrant cultural scene and the rhythms of the surrounding Manhattan neighborhood. His *Film No. 18* (better known as *Mahagonny*) was a laborious project that took the form of a four-channel film alternating between different categories of images, including portraits of fellow Chelsea residents, canted shots of New York traffic, landscapes, nature, and string figures. A city symphony of sorts, these sequences of images were set to Kurt Weill and Bertolt Brecht's opera *Rise and Fall of the City of Mahagonny*.[3]

Another lesser discussed figure who was crucial to the Chelsea's flourishing visual cultures is Shirley Clarke. An occupant of the hotel's penthouse space, Clarke formed the TeePee Video Space Troupe in the late 1960s, naming the group after the shape of the hotel roof's apex, under which they worked. Clarke and her troupe formed a workshop, experimenting artistically by placing televisions in various totemlike configurations, assembling monitors into sculptures, and mixing the moving image with "low-tech materials" such as paper and paint. Clarke's ludic experiments challenged both notions of aesthetic seriousness and frustrated goal-orienting understandings of the artistic process, and the participants of these workshops were a heterogeneous and constantly evolving group of filmmakers, dancers, and artists. Implicit within the moving image assemblages of the TeePee Video Space Troupe, then, was a valorization of community and mutability, a hospitality toward guests and a receptivity to contingency and change that rhymed with the ideals of the community of artists dwelling in the rooms below.

While practical considerations account, in part, for the limited reception of and critical engagement with these filmmakers' works (Clarke's projects were often site-specific and ephemeral, and it was not uncommon for an irascible Smith to destroy film reels, even mid-screening), I am nonetheless tempted to consider the fate of the Chelsea's minor cinemas within broader frames of cultural and economic value. Mirroring the market forces that would ultimately lead to the Chelsea's precipitous decline, the experimental films produced in the hotel's golden age have been met by one of two fates. Work by household names—think of Warhol's *Chelsea Girls*—would over time become consecrated, dutifully preserved for future generations, while others would pale into relative obscurity. Call it a logic of compound interest.

* * *

I first encountered Clarke's work by way of Amélie van Elmbt and Maya Duverdier's documentary *Dreaming Walls: Inside the Chelsea Hotel* (2022), which combines archival footage of the hotel in its former splendor with intimate portraits of the "holdouts," the last remaining long-term tenants, for whom the building's protracted renovation has become part of their daily lives. While the film's release coincided with the reopening of the hotel after over a decade of work, *Dreaming Walls* is not uncritical of the redevelopment. The film evokes the sad fate of the Chelsea following an uncertain couple of decades. (When the hotel's board of directors ousted Bard as manager in 2007, this marked an inflection point, and the ensuing years have represented both a protracted legal battle between the new owners and "legacy" tenants protected by state rent regulations, as well as a more symbolic struggle over the soul of the building). *Dreaming Walls* joins a growing body of documentary films on the hotel, mounting a muted critique of the logics of expropriation and gentrification with which the hotel is now synonymous. If Abel Ferrara's 2009 documentary presented a vision of the *Chelsea on the Rocks*, then van Elmbt and Duverdier lingers with the rubble, patiently excavating the fallout from the hotel's recent mismanagement. Here, the hallowed halls of the past meet the hollowed-out walls of the present.

In the introduction to this book I invoked, via Jacques Derrida, a tension between two notions of hospitality: a former idealized understanding of the term entails an imperative to welcome the other (*an ethics of hospitality*), while a latter contractual understanding is primarily motivated by economic interests (or *hospitality as industry*). The case of the Chelsea, an establishment in which long-term dwellers cohabited with temporary drifters, starkly illustrates these two opposing forces. While Bard was often reproached for tending toward the former understanding of hospitality (his mantra of "cheap rooms, fun people, flexible management" ran contrary to good business sense), the Chelsea's new management structure represents an economic course correction. As *Dreaming Walls* shows us, the holdouts inhabit a paradoxical and interstitial position within the hotel's new incarnation insofar as their symbolic value (as living connections to a receding past) drastically outweighs their economic might. As one resident explains, the new blueprint for the hotel includes a separate elevator for long-term residents, an extension of the logic of the "poor doors" already ubiquitous in Manhattan, which phobically triage people along lines of socioeconomic status. Circulating in the hotel's imaginary but ushered off to the side—heard of, but not necessarily seen—the long-term residents are akin to ghosts.

Ghosts abound in *Dreaming Walls*. As a construction worker notes to long-term resident Merle Lister, "There's a lot of history in this building, it's a lot of ghosts going on round here." In an early scene we enter a darkened room that has been gutted. The camera pans to reveal a bathtub, a blue tiled surround; part of the wall is removed to show an exposed cavity. This is the imperfect canvas onto which the directors project an image of Nico, a Warhol superstar, in footage from *Chelsea Girls*. In another shot a dilapidated room with peeling wallpaper provides a fitting texture against which to present footage of Patti Smith. Grungy aesthetics meld with dingy surroundings; archival fragments, chipped paint, and cracked

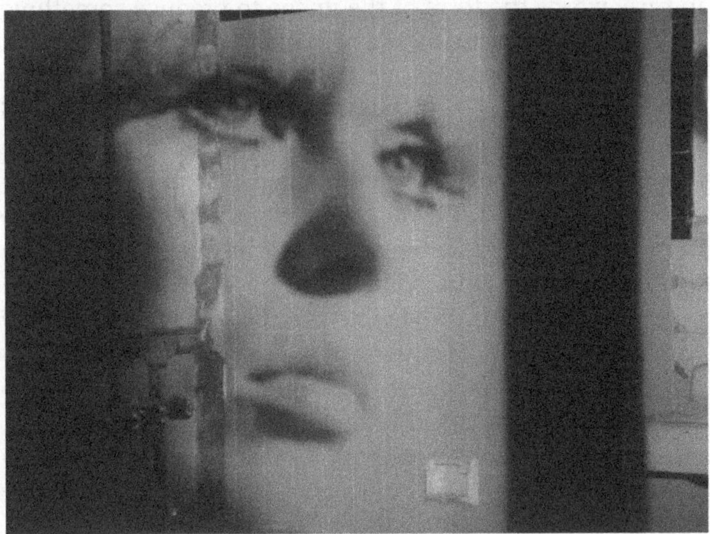

walls coalesce into something approaching a scrapbook or zine, harking back to earlier forms of (counter)cultural dissemination. These scenes, in which the cinematic "dream screen" is reprojected onto the "dreaming walls" of the film's title, registers a debt to Mekas, who made use of similar techniques during his famed live performances. While it is the degraded surface, the blotchy, crackled patina of vintage film stock that typically acts as a visual index of historicity or obsolescence, the pockmarked images that we encounter here are the unique effects of the encounter between cinema and the hotel. In this visual experiment the ghostly frames merge with the rough canvas of the hotel walls to yield a hybrid multimedial image.

As the luminescent glow of the cinematic image extends over the building's surfaces, and its rough, uneven texture, in turn, warps the form of the image to produce something new, I find a new articulation of the contours of the idea that has informed this book: that like the cinema, the hotel functions as a medium. Both stand at the crossroads of art and industry; both aggregate audiences along various (socioeconomic, aesthetic) axes; and both entail complex—often concealed—labors of mise-en-scène and performance to ensure that their intended audiences enjoy the spectacle. Cinema and the hotel are twinned media that traffic in ideas of fantasy, projection, and invisible labor. By taking a journey through the history of cinema by way of its spaces of temporary dwelling, we encounter a range of spheres and scales—public and private, local and global—and affective states, ranging from the toil of labor to the effortlessness of leisurely pursuits, from the inertia of space-time compression to the tedium of the self-same and the eroticism of the no-strings-attached encounter.

While my summoning of the ghosts of the Chelsea Hotel might strike some readers as a somber note on which to close this book, I do not read van Elmbt and Duverdier's projections as a melancholy encomium, a stubborn affective orientation toward recuperation, or an impossible call to salvage a past that now lies in ruins. Rather, I find in the act of cinematic projection any number of gateways or open doors that might hospitably beckon us toward the hotel's rich and vibrant lifeworlds, both past and present.

Acknowledgments

An unexpected pleasure that I found when writing a book about the hotel in cinema is that whenever I was asked the dreaded question of what I was working on, I would not fail to leave the conversation without filling a new page of my weather-beaten notepad. To think about the generative topic and topos of the hotel is, fittingly, an invitation to sociality—and so it brings me great pleasure to revisit those notepad scrawls, and the accumulation of debts to which they attest, to thank the many friends and colleagues that helped along the way. I thank Erika Balsom and Genevieve Yue for seeing the potential of this book in its early stages, and for their superlative care and attention in seeing it through to completion. I am grateful to John David Rhodes, a cherished friend and colleague, who continues to open up new and exciting ways to think about cinematic space. I thank the Master and Fellows of St John's College, Cambridge, for the necessary time and means to write this book, and Georgina Evans in particular for her continued support. Many thanks are due to Victoria Baena, Ferdinando Cocco, Jacob Engelberg, Daria Ezerova, Elena Gorfinkel, Damien Pollard, Brian Price, B. Ruby Rich, Lili Owen Rowlands, Rani Singh, Kyle Stevens, Rebecca Sugden, McNeil Taylor, Sylvana Tomaselli, James S. Williams, and Emma Wilson. Thank you to James Cahill and Pamela Wojcik for their generous and constructive reviews of this manuscript, as well as Thomas Lay and his editorial team at Fordham University Press, who provided expert help at important critical junctures.

The idea for this book first came to me in the space that would ultimately become its subject: a hotel room, during a conference a couple of years ago. Lying by my side then, and by my side now, is Samuel Bell, whose continued love and support has helped this book see the light of day.

Notes

1. I Can't Sleep

1 Charles Simic, "The Congress of Insomniacs," in *Hotel Insomnia* (Orlando, FL: Harcourt, 1992), 2.

2 Wayne Koestenbaum, *Hotel Theory* (New York: Soft Skull Press, 2007), 7.

3 See John David Rhodes, *Spectacle of Property: The House in American Film* (Minneapolis: University of Minnesota Press, 2017); Pamela Robertson Wojcik, *The Apartment Plot: Urban Living in American Film and Popular Culture, 1945 to 1975* (Durham, NC: Duke University Press, 2010); and Merrill Schleier, *Skyscraper Cinema* (Minneapolis: University of Minnesota Press, 2009).

4 Koestenbaum, *Hotel Theory*, 12.

5 For an analysis of multiplot hotel narratives see chapter 3 of this book, as well as Yvette Blackwood, "Parallel Hotel Worlds," in *Moving Pictures/Stopping Places*, ed. David B. Clarke, Valerie Crawford Pfannhauser, and Marcus A. Doel (Lanham, MD: Lexington, 2009), 277–96.

6 See Jacques Derrida, "Hostipitality," *Angelaki: Journal of the Theoretical Humanities* 5, no. 3 (December 2000): 3.

7 See Cyril Aouizarate and Gabrielle Halpern, *Penser l'hospitalité: L'artisan hotelier et la philosophe* (La Tour d'Aigues: Editions de l'Aube, 2022). The idea of the hotel as both "housing" and "reflecting" a shifting society at large takes on another dimension in the recent context of COVID-19, in which vacant hotels were used to house homeless populations.

8 Serge Kaganski, "Amélie pas jolie," *Libération*, May 31, 2001, https://www.liberation.fr/cinema/2001/05/31/amelie-pas-jolie_366387/

9 Claire Denis's films are likely to remind us of the limits of predetermining what hotel spaces can be and do. In *I Can't Sleep*, the presence

of a murderer and the fraught social positionality of the protagonists might lead us to preempt the affective tone of the film. Yet we are led not necessarily toward the realm of horror that we might expect but into a narrative space that is subtle, dedramatized, and even surprisingly tender. Contrast this with *Trouble Every Day* (2001), in which we follow an American couple, Shane and June Brown, on a honeymoon trip to Paris. We encounter them first midair, sipping champagne on their flight, before making their way to a prestigious grand hotel overlooking Opéra. We soon learn that Shane's real aim is not to indulge in sightseeing but to track down an old colleague from a mysterious science project gone awry and his vampiric wife, Coré. Following his encounter with the vampire, he grows increasingly detached from his new wife before brutally assaulting the maid who cleans his room as the film comes to a close. Reading these films side by side, the hotel emerges as a rich space in which the ambivalence of social relations—and the horror of adjacency—can be explored. For illuminating reading of these films, see Andrew Asibong, "Claire Denis's Flickering Spaces of Hospitality," *L'esprit créateur* 51, no. 1 (Spring 2011): 154–67; and Nikolaj Lübecker, "The Dedramatization of Violence in Claire Denis's *I Can't Sleep*," *Paragraph* 30, no. 2 (2007): 17–33.

10 Frieda Grafe, "Die saubere Architektur in Gefahr: Die Grandhotels in der Unterhaltungsindustrie," in *Ungenierte Unterhaltung mit Frieda Grafe im Grandhotel*, ed. Karola Gramann, Ute Holl, and Heide Schlüpmann (Vienna: Synema, 2022), 61. My translation.

11 Grafe, "Die saubere Architektur in Gefahr," 61.

12 See "The Paradiso Experience," *mk*2 Hotel Paradiso, January 2021, https://www.mk2hotelparadiso.com/en/page/philosophy-hotels-paris-12th.11700.html

13 Elena Gorfinkel, "Somnolent Screens," *Sight and Sound* 28, no. 6 (June 2018): 14–15; See also Roland Barthes, "Leaving the Movie Theater," in *The Rustle of Language*, trans. Richard Howard (New York: Farrar, Strauss and Giroux, 1986).

14 See Roland Barthes, *How to Live Together: Novelistic Simulations of Some Everyday Spaces*, trans. Katie Briggs (New York: Columbia University Press, 2014).

15 I borrow this phrase from Caetlin Benson-Allott's excellent study *The Stuff of Spectatorship: Material Cultures of Film and Television* (Oakland: University of California Press, 2021). Benson-Allott's book advances a compelling argument that film theorists ought to reattune their perception toward those details of the spectatorial experience that are too often relegated to the realm of the epiphenomenal.
16 Rhodes, *Spectacle of Property*, 13.
17 Grafe, "Die saubere Architektur in Gefahr," 61.
18 I borrow this term from Mark Katz's "The Hotel Kracauer," *differences: A Journal of Feminist Cultural Studies* 11, no. 2 (Summer 1999): 146.
19 Theodor Adorno, *Minima Moralia: Reflections on a Damaged Life*, trans. E. F. N. Jephcott (London: Verso, 2005), 117.
20 Henry James, *The American Scene* (London: Granville, 1987), 73.
21 Fredric Jameson, *Postmodernism, Or the Cultural Logic of Late Capitalism* (Durham, NC: Duke University Press, 1991), 38–39. Perhaps not surprisingly, critic John Needham, in his collection of essays *Departure Lounge*, described an experience of the same hotel in very different terms. John Needham, *Departure Lounge: Travel and Literature in the Post Modern World* (London: Carnacet, 1999), 4. As the book's dustjacket notes, *Departure Lounge* is a self-described exercise in "testing theory against the thing that it theorizes."

2. Labor, Leisure, and Visual Pleasure

1 Not insignificantly, this revolving door is manually powered by a doorman, thereby foreshadowing a job that (much like Jannings's character) would soon become redundant.
2 For a fuller account of this history, see Klaus Kreimeier, *The Ufa Story: A History of Germany's Greatest Film Company, 1918–1945*, trans. Robert and Rita Kimber (Berkeley: University of California Press, 1999), 144–45.
3 Georgie Carr, "Ruben Östlund's 'Triangle of Sadness,'" *Another Gaze*, October 27, 2022, https://www.anothergaze.com/georgie-carr-ruben-ostlunds-triangle-sadness/

4 Egoyan cited in "Emotional Logic, an Interview with Mark Glassman," *Speaking Parts* (Toronto: Coach House Press, 1993), 172.

5 Egoyan cited in Hamid Naficy, *An Accented Cinema: Exilic and Diasporic Filmmaking* (Princeton, NJ: Princeton University Press, 2001), 252–53.

6 Claire Denis, who shares Egoyan's interests in drift, desire, and exile, has previously spoken about a never-realized joint project that she envisaged with Egoyan and Olivier Assayas that revolves around the space of the hotel. See Judith Mayne, *Claire Denis* (Champaign: University of Illinois Press, 2005), 108–9.

7 See Paul Virilio and Atom Egoyan, "Video Letters," in *Atom Egoyan*, ed. Carol Desbarats, Jacinto Lageira, Danièle Rivière, and Paul Virilio, trans. Brian Holmes (Paris: Editions Dis Voir, 1993).

8 See Carol Wolkowitz, *Bodies at Work* (London: Sage Publications, 2005), 153–61.

9 Elena Gorfinkel, "The Body's Failed Labor: Performance Work in Sexploitation Cinema," *Framework: The Journal of Cinema and Media* 53, no. 1 (Spring 2012): 81.

10 Emma Wilson, *Atom Egoyan* (Champaign: University of Illinois Press, 2009), 36.

11 Ibid.

12 While Avilés is interested in staging a story of interclass proximity, she resists rehashing unlikely stories of social ascendancy of the kind we find in a Wayne Wang's blockbuster hit *Maid in Manhattan* (2003), in which a Latina maid in a luxury hotel (Jennifer Lopez) is mistaken for a guest.

13 Caroline Field Levander and Matthew Pratt Guterl, *Hotel Life: The Story of a Place Where Anything Can Happen* (Chapel Hill: University of North Carolina Press, 2015), 104.

14 John David Rhodes, *Spectacle of Property: The House in American Film* (Minneapolis: University of Minnesota Press, 2017), 131.

15 Jacques Rancière, *Proletarian Nights* (New York: Verso, 2012), 64.

16 Gabriel Rockhill, "Rancière's Productive Contradictions," *Symposium* 15, no. 2 (2011): 41.

17 See Salomé Aguilera Skvirsky, "Must the Subaltern Speak? On Roma and the Cinema of Domestic Service," *Forma* 1, no. 2 (2020): 1–34.

18 Norman Klein cited in Erik Morse, "Hotel Theory: The History of the Los Angeles Hotel," *Los Angeles Review of Books*, October 2012, https://lareviewofbooks.org/article/hotel-theory-the-history-of-the-los-angeles-hotel/.
19 Bruce Bégout, *Common Place: The American Motel* (Los Angeles: Otis Books, 2010).
20 Ibid.
21 See Barbara Ehrenreich, *Nickel and Dimed: On Not Getting by in Low Wage America* (London: Granta, 2001).
22 Michael Sorkin, "See You in Disneyland," *Design Quarterly* 154 (Winter 1992): 6; Jean Baudrillard, *Simulacra and Simulation*, trans. Sheila Faria Glaser (Ann Arbor: University of Michigan Press, 1994), 12;
23 Jean-Louis Comolli, "Mechanical Bodies, Ever More Heavenly," trans. Annette Michelson, *October* 83 (Winter 1998): 19.

3. Lost in Space

1 Rem Koolhaas, *Delirious New York* (New York: Monacelli Press, 1994), 148.
2 Ibid., 150.
3 Pamela Robertson Wojcik, *The Apartment Plot: Urban Living in American Film and Popular Culture, 1945 to 1975* (Durham, NC: Duke University Press, 2010), 3.
4 See Siegfried Kracauer, "The Hotel Lobby," in *The Mass Ornament: Weimar Essays* (Cambridge, MA: Harvard University Press, 1995), 173–86.
5 On Resnais's *Last Year at Marienbad* as an easy target for art cinema's excesses, see Rosalind Galt and Karl Schoonover, "Introduction: The Impurity of Art Cinema," in *Global Art Cinema: New Theories and Histories* (Oxford: Oxford University Press, 2010), 16.
6 See Gilles Deleuze, *Cinema II: The Time Image* (London: Bloomsbury, 2013 [1985]), 108.
7 Consider, for example, Wong Kar-wai's *Chungking Express* (1994) and Olivier Assayas's *Demonlover* (2002).
8 Caroline Field Levander and Matthew Pratt Guterl, *Hotel Life: The Story of a Place Where Anything Can Happen* (Chapel Hill: University of North Carolina Press, 2015), 104, 107.

9 Fredric Jameson, *Postmodernism: Or, the Cultural Logic of Late Capitalism* (Durham, NC: Duke University Press, 1991), 43. Arguably, much of the difficulty of locating the entrances and exits of the Bonaventure can be ascribed to the uneven redevelopment of downtown Los Angeles. For a critique of Jameson's reading of the Bonaventure, see John Needham, *Departure Lounge: Travel and Literature in the Post Modern World* (London: Carnacet, 1999).
10 Jameson, *Postmodernism*, 44.
11 Anna Backman Rodgers, *Sofia Coppola: The Politics of Visual Pleasure* (Oxford: Berghahn, 2019), 104.
12 Ibid.
13 Suzanne Ferriss, *Lost in Translation* (London: BFI, 2023), 47.
14 Homay King, *Lost in Translation: Orientalism, Cinema, and the Enigmatic Signifier* (Durham, NC: Duke University Press, 2010), 149.
15 Levander and Guterl, *Hotel Life*, 107.
16 Ibid., 108.
17 Robert A. Davidson, *The Hotel: Occupied Space* (Toronto: University of Toronto Press, 2018), 83.
18 See Sara Ahmed, *Queer Phenomenology: Objects, Orientations, Others* (Durham, NC: Duke University Press, 2006).
19 Sofia Coppola cited in "Finding Japan in Lost in Translation," *Focus Features*, August 23, 2019, https://www.focusfeatures.com/article/film-locations_japan_lost-in-translation.
20 See Rem Koolhaas, *Generic City* (Sassenheim, The Netherlands: Sikkens Foundation, 1995).
21 King, *Lost in Translation*, 167.
22 Thomas C. Carlson, "The Comeback Corpse in Hollywood: *Mystery Train*, True Romance, and the Politics of Elvis in the '90s," *Popular Music and Society* 22, no. 2 (1998): 2.
23 bell hooks, *Reel to Real: Race, Class and Sex in the Movies* (London: Routledge, 1996), 124.
24 Ibid.
25 Yvette Blackwood, "Parallel Hotel Worlds," in *Moving Pictures/Stopping Places*, ed. David B. Clarke, Valerie Crawford Pfannhauser, and Marcus A. Doel (Lanham, MD: Lexington, 2009), 281.

4. Love Hotel

1 Geoff Dyer, "Sex and Hotels," in *Otherwise Known as the Human Condition: Selected Essays and Reviews, 1989–2010* (Minneapolis: Graywolf, 2011), 315–18. Dyer's description of a guest's "moral weightlessness" indeed resonates with my earlier discussion in chapter 2 of how hotels encourage their occupants to remain incurious about the labor conditions that underpin these establishments.

2 Elizabeth Johnson, "Love Hotels, Japan," in *New Hotels for Global Nomads*, ed. Donald Albrecht (London: Merrell, 2003), 135.

3 Jean Nouvel, "A Sensual Anthology," https://www.jeannouvel.com/en/projects/the-hotel/.

4 The references to cinema in his architecture range from full-scale projects (ambitious, though unrealized, plans for Venice's Palazzo del Cinema) through to signature details (the tiles covering Paris's Institut du Monde Arabe that respond to light levels and function like a camera's aperture).

5 Brigitte Metra, cited in the documentary *Jean Nouvel: Aesthetics of Wonder* (dir. Beat Kuert, 1998).

6 Johnson, "Love Hotels, Japan," 135. To extend Nouvel's frame of cinematic reference, the spatial logic that Albrecht describes recalls a moment in Busby Berkeley's pre-Code classic *Gold Diggers of 1933*. Following a downpour of rain in the "Pettin' in the Park" musical number, the female dancers take shelter in a gridlike structure that recalls both a corridor-style hotel layout and a strip of film. With the lowering of a curtain we see the silhouettes of bodies undressing within these rigid cell-like structures. A mischievous boy with a lascivious grin (Billy Barty) gets his hands on the curtain pulley. To his disappointment, however, they are wearing metal party frocks. In its thwarting of the expectations of nude flesh, this visual gag provides a rejoinder to philosopher Stanley Cavell's suggestion that "A woman in a movie is *dressed* . . . hence potentially undressed." See *The World Viewed: Reflections on the Ontology of Film* (Cambridge, MA: Harvard University Press, 1979), 44, original emphasis.

7 I borrow the term "pornotopia" from Steven Marcus, who uses it to describe the ways in which spatial relations are governed by a

pornographic imaginary. See his *The Other Victorians: A Study of Sexuality and Pornography in Mid-Nineteenth-Century England* (London: Corgi, 1964), 268–74.

8 Neville Wakefield, *Jeff Burton: Untitled*, (Tokyo: Composite Press, 1998).

9 Jennifer Wicke cited in Gorfinkel, "'Dated Sexuality': Anna Biller's Viva and the Retrospective Life of Sexploitation Cinema," *Camera Obscura* 78 (2011): 98.

10 Ibid.

11 See Laura Mulvey, "Visual Pleasure and Narrative Cinema," *Screen* 16, no. 3, (October 1975): 6–11. Justin Remes writes convincingly of how the promiscuous interplay between presence and absence in the film—what he calls its "peekaboo effect"—offers us a fresh understanding of erotic cinema's visual syntax. See his discussion of Uman and Mulvey in chapter 3 of *Absence in Cinema: The Art of Showing Nothing* (New York: Columbia University Press, 2020), 106–77; see also Remes, "Animated Holes: An Interview with Naomi Uman," *Millennium Film Journal* 66 (2017): 68–72.

12 Indeed, for Geoff Dyer there is significant appeal in closing the loop between these two stages in the life of pornographic media: "Ideally, to square the circle, the porno you watch in your hotel room will be set in a hotel room." "Sex and Hotels," 318.

13 In Japan, the term "pink movie" is used as an umbrella term to refer to a number of forms of "softer" adult material such as erotic thrillers and sexploitation films that traffic in nudity and sexual titillation.

14 "Modern Living: Sinerama in Osaka," *Time*, March 22, 1971, content.time.com/time/subscriber/article/0,33009,904934,00.html.

15 Peter Alilunas, *Smutty Little Movies: The Creation and Regulation of Adult Video* (Oakland: University of California Press, 2016), 56, 51.

16 For an account of this phenomenon, see Lauren Rabinowitz, *For the Love of Pleasure Women, Movies, and Culture in Turn-of-the-century Chicago* (New Brunswick, NJ: Rutgers University Press, 1998), 82–84, as well as Sarah Keller, "Cinephobia: To Wonder, To Worry," *LOLA* 5 (2014), https://www.lolajournal.com/5/cinephobia.html.

17 I am drawing on Judith Mayne's apt phrasing a propos of the through-the-keyhole drama in *The Woman at the Keyhole: Feminism and Women's Cinema* (Bloomington: Indiana University Press, 1990), 178.

18 For an extended reading of the film via Gustave Courbet, see Chris Norris, "The Origin of the World," *Film Comment* 46, no. 5 (September/October 2010), 26–30.
19 I am thinking here of Stan Brakhage's 1971 autopsy film *The Act of Seeing With One's Own Eyes*, which explores bodily interiors, albeit in a different register.
20 There exists a long tradition of feminist critiques of Stan Brakhage's cinematic practice by fellow experimental filmmakers such as Marjorie Keller (see her 1977 film *Misconception*) and Carolee Schneemann, whose essay "It Is Painting" draws attention to the gendered blind spots in Brakhage's work. That essay is in *Stan Brakhage: Filmmaker*, ed. David E. James (Philadelphia: Temple University Press, 2005), 78–87.
21 This point is expanded upon in, for example, Meg Morley's review of the film shortly after its release. See "Les Rendez-vous d'Anna (Chantal Akerman)," *Camera Obscura* 3–4 (1979): 214.
22 Marion Schmid, *Chantal Akerman* (Manchester: Manchester University Press, 2010), 57; B. Ruby Rich, *Chick Flicks: Theories and Memories of the Feminist Film Movement* (Durham, NC: Duke University Press, 1998), 172. For a brilliant discussion of proximity and distance in this scene, see also Christine Smallwood, *La Captive* (Berlin: Fireflies Press, 2024).

5. Chelsea Ghosts

1 James Leo Cahill, "What Remains, What Returns: Garbage, Ghosts, and the Two Ends of Cinema," in *Ends of Cinema*, ed. Richard Grusin and Jocelyn Szczepaniak-Gillece (Minneapolis: University of Minnesota Press, 2020), 85.
2 For an authoritative account of this history see Sherill Tippins, *Inside the Dream Palace: The Life and Times of New York's Legendary Chelsea Hotel* (London: Simon & Schuster, 2013).
3 A fuller account of this film can be found in chapter 9 of John Szwed's *Cosmic Scholar: The Life and Times of Harry Smith* (New York: Farrar, Straus and Giroux, 2023).

18 For an extended reading of the film via Gustave Courbet, see Chris [illegible], "The Origin of the World," Film Comment 46, no. 5 (September/October 2010), 38–40.

19 I am thinking here of Stan Brakhage's [illegible] [illegible] in The Act of Seeing With One's Own Eyes, which explores bodily interiors albeit in a different [illegible].

20 [illegible] [illegible] [illegible] of Stan [illegible] [illegible] [illegible] fellow experimental filmmakers such as Marjorie [illegible] [illegible] film Mirror [illegible] and Carolee Schneemann [illegible] [illegible] [illegible] [illegible] [illegible] [illegible] [illegible] [illegible] [illegible] [illegible] Stan Brakhage's work [illegible] [illegible] Filmmakers [illegible] [illegible] [illegible] [illegible] Press, 20[illegible]).

21 [illegible] [illegible] [illegible] [illegible] [illegible] [illegible] [illegible] [illegible] [illegible] [illegible] [illegible] [illegible] Anne [illegible] [illegible] [illegible].

22 [illegible] Sarah [illegible] [illegible] [illegible] [illegible] [illegible] [illegible] [illegible] [illegible] Theory and Practice [illegible] Film [illegible] [illegible] [illegible], NC: Duke University Press [illegible], 1[illegible]. For a [illegible] [illegible] [illegible] [illegible] [illegible] [illegible] [illegible] [illegible] [illegible] [illegible] [illegible] Press, 2[illegible]).

5 [illegible]

1 [illegible] [illegible] [illegible] [illegible] [illegible] [illegible] [illegible] [illegible] [illegible] [illegible] [illegible] [illegible] [illegible] [illegible] [illegible] [illegible] (Minneapolis: University of Minnesota Press, 2020), 5[illegible].

2 [illegible] [illegible] [illegible] [illegible] [illegible] [illegible] [illegible] [illegible] [illegible] [illegible] [illegible] [illegible] [illegible] [illegible] [illegible] [illegible] [illegible].

3 [illegible] [illegible] [illegible] [illegible] [illegible] [illegible] [illegible] [illegible] [illegible] Cosmic Scream: [illegible] [illegible] [illegible] [illegible] (New York: [illegible] [illegible] and [illegible], 20[illegible]).

Figures

Index

Jules O'Dwyer is Teaching Associate in Film Studies and French at the University of Cambridge. He is the author of *The Seduction of Space: Cruising French Cinema* (2025).

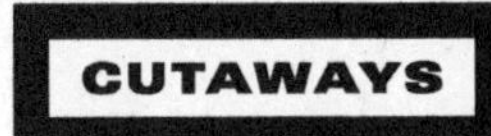

SERIES EDITORS:
Erika Balsom (King's College London)
and **Genevieve Yue** (The New School)

Elena Gorfinkel, John David Rhodes, *The Prop*

Jules O'Dwyer, *Hotels*